KENTUCKY 1800, BARREN COUNTY TAX BOOK

Copyright 23 February 2021
Stemmons Publishing
1078 Shields Lane
South Jordan, Utah 84095

BIBLIOGRAPHY FOR KENTUCKY 1800, BARREN COUNTY TAX BOOK

United States, Department of State, compiled and edited by Clarence Edwin Carter, *The Territorial Papers of the United States* Washington, D.C.: Government Printing Office, 1934-1962. 26 volumes. National Archives microfilm publications: M0721

vol. 1. The Territorial Papers of the United States, General.
vols. II & III The Territory Northwest of the River Ohio, 1787-1803.
vol. IV The Territory South of the River Ohio, 1790-1796.
vols. V & VI The Territory of Mississippi, 1798-1817.
vols. VII & VIII The Territory of Indiana, 1800-1816.
vol. IX The Territory of Orleans, 1803-1812.
vols. X - XII The Territory of Michigan, 1805-1837.
vols. XIII - XV The Territory of Louisiana-Missouri, 1803-1821.
vols. XVI & XVII The Territory of Illinois, 1809-1818.
vol. XVIII The Territory of Alabama, 1817-1819.
vols. XIX - XXI The Territory of Arkansas, 1819-1836.
vols. XXII - XXVI The Territory of Florida, 1821-1845.

[Please note: *Larger lists of names, such as petitions, etc., will be included. Names from regular governmental/public transactions that contain no individual biographical details will not.*

INTRODUCTION TO KENTUCKY 1800 TAX LISTS

The county location refers to the locality of the acreage listed on the tax list. If the person has none listed, then there will be no county entered. This does not mean they don't live in that county. Their county of residence can be surmised from the source listing which county tax list their information is obtained from. Sometimes the list for one county will include acreage located in another county.

KY-01 **KENTUCKY 1800, BARREN COUNTY TAX BOOK.** It contains 494 names from the Barren County tax list and 1 from *The Territorial Papers of the U.S.* Even though the 1800 census is missing this list provides an amazing amount of information that substitutes nicely for that missing census, including white and black males aged 16-21 and those 21 and over. This is the kind of information one would expect to find on the census for that period. This list includes all taxable heads of household. Some additional biographical details may be included, plus possible relationships with other family members. The names of the blacks may be found in court, land, and probate records. For information on how to obtain this book search by the title or "Books by John Stemmons" at Amazon.com. This comes automatically with a paperback binding.

INDEXES

Indexes are expensive to compile.

Which is why many books do not have them. Most that do just have a simple name index. A noteworthy exception is the *Territorial Papers of the United States* which gives some limited context as explained below.

Indexes are expensive but using modern technology we at Stemmons Publishing have included nearly all the context you may need. 100% context is probably not possible such as in a census that lists multiple neighbors. Search for entries of the same page in our book(s) or the original document if you require more information.

PUBLICATIONS FROM STEMMONS PUBLISHING

These following publications are not just traditional alphabetical lists of names, they include the context of information with each name!!

Why is that so important? Because many of the names in our books were obtained from various sources including South Carolina jury lists, the *Territorial Papers of the United States* (28 volumes each with its own index), petitions, tax lists, etc., and like most books with indexes common names require a lot of time to check each entry in the index. Can you imagine how many Smiths you would have to go through page-by-page for a compilation the size of *Territorial Papers of the United States*? Their indexes provide some context such as signing a petition. No explanation is given of what, when, or why the petition was made. Because we have included the context with each name, you can easily search all the Smiths, Taylors, Browns, Williams, etc., without all the drudgery! And since most of us have common surnames, we may need some help. Now, the originals of the South Carolina jury lists are housed in the South Carolina Department of Archives and History. Therefore, you may not have access to the originals. The way we index names means it is almost as good as being at the Archives yourself and doubly so since these documents are loose papers and do not have an original index. Our books provide an enhanced way of using *Territorial Papers of the United States* that the original compilers did not envision. So, if you have this collection, your obtaining our books compiled from those volumes will help your access to *Territorial Papers of the United States* even if you are not interested in our books about South Carolina jury lists. Now, that's what I call achieving the potential of a real index! It takes the bare skeleton of a name on a list and covers it with the flesh, hair, eyes, etc., of a human body. The names are more able to stand alone by themselves than is the case with a traditional index. We did not index subjects. *Territorial Papers of the United States* did.

Checking a name from our books and going to the page in *Territorial Papers of the United States* will show the list of names. Those listed next to the person of interest may be neighbors and relatives.

Guidelines for Entry of Names

Many times, names have been difficult to decipher. Other times, the document itself has been damaged in various ways that impacted our ability to read the information. Several methods have been employed to indicate to the reader when we had difficulty. They are as follows:

When a surname has been difficult to determine and could be read alternately, we have indicated this by using two and sometimes three possibilities. For example, Rud or Ried. For your convenience we have made separate entries for each possibility: Rud or Ried and Ried or Rud. We encourage individuals to go to the original source and make a determination for themselves if the name is important for their research. For given names, we will also indicate more than one possibility, but will not make separate entries for each one.

When an undetermined number of letters were unreadable, we used the ellipsis ". . ." in place of the letters we could not decipher, while we included those characters we could read. For example: Cr . . . [surname] and . . . seph [given name]. It would be difficult to determine the surname with confidence, but the given name is most likely "Joseph".

When a known number of characters could not be read, an asterisk "*" was used in place of each letter we could not decipher. Often the name can be determined based on where the asterisk is placed. For example, with Brow* one can readily determine the name is most likely Brown. However, when one or more asterisks are placed at the beginning of a name, the possibilities become more numerous and therefore difficult to determine.

When we were unsure about the reading, we would include a question mark "?" after the name.

Sometimes we could not read the name because the writing was too faint, it was covered with ink blotches, portions of the document was damaged/missing, or for many other reasons. We tried to indicate this when we felt a name was there by using "[Unreadable]", "[Missing]", "[Illegible]", "[Name crossed out]", etc., in place of the name. In some cases, a name might be read by examining carefully the original document.

When the first letter was obviously wrong and would interfere in a researcher's ability to readily see the name, we have placed in brackets what we thought the name should be along with the spelling of the name in the original. One can use the search feature on the Internet to find these names. An example is Knewkurk [Newkirk], Richard. A researcher might never know to look under the spelling Knewkurk and therefore miss potentially vital information. By searching for the name Newkirk, one would find this entry.

Sometimes it is difficult to tell which is the given name and which is the surname. When there has been doubt about the proper order of given name/surname, we have made an entry such as: Everet or Jones, [surname], and Jones or Everet [given name]. Then we have made another entry with the names reversed such as Jones or Everet [surname], and Everet or Jones [given name].

When deciphering entries, we have always tried to err on the side of reasonable, known, practical, and possible names rather than unreasonable, impossible, or impractical spellings.

495 Names

Adams, John P.,   Kentucky   Barren County
       Adams, John P.,   Male
The entry for land owned by Walter Courts was in his name.
Barren County Tax Book, 1800, part 1 - page: 4
FAMILY HISTORY LIBRARY film 7865
Alfred or Ansel, Ansel or Alfred,   Kentucky   Barren County
       Alfred or Ansel, Ansel or Alfred, over 21 Male   **Color:** White
Acres of land: 200; Barren Co.; watercourse: Skeggs Creek; Entry: Ansel Alfred; Survey: same; Patents: 0; white males over 21: 1; white males 16-21: 0; blacks over 16: 0; total blacks: 0; horses: 18; stud horses: 0; retail stores: 0; tavern license: 0.
Barren County Tax Book, 1800, part 1 - page: 1
FAMILY HISTORY LIBRARY film 7865
Allen, Charles,   Kentucky   Barren County
       Allen, Charles, over 21 Male   **Color:** White
       Allen, 16-21 Male   **Color:** White
Acres of land: 100; Barren Co.; watercourse: Beaver Creek; Entry: Bird Henrick; Survey: same; Patents: same; white males over 21: 1; white males 16-21: 1; blacks over 16: 0; total blacks: 0; horses: 1; stud horses: 0; retail stores: 0; tavern license: 0.
Barren County Tax Book, 1800, part 1 - page: 1
FAMILY HISTORY LIBRARY film 7865
Aller, David,   Kentucky   Barren County
       Aller, David,   over 21 Male   **Color:** White
Acres of land: 150; Barren Co.; watercourse: Beaver Creek; Entry: David Aller; Survey: same; Patents: 0; white males over 21: 1; white males 16-21: 0; blacks over 16: 0; total blacks: 0; horses: 5; stud horses: 0; retail stores: 0; tavern license: 0.

Barren County Tax Book, 1800, part 1 - page: 1
FAMILY HISTORY LIBRARY film 7865
Amberson, Johnson,   Kentucky   Barren County
       Amberson, Johnson,   over 21 Male
       Color: White
Acres of land: 0; Barren Co.; watercourse: 0; Entry: 0; Survey: 0; Patents: 0; white males over 21: 1; white males 16-21: 0; blacks over 16: 0; total blacks: 0; horses: 0; stud horses: 0; retail stores: 0; tavern license: 0.
Barren County Tax Book, 1800, part 1 - page: 1
FAMILY HISTORY LIBRARY film 7865
Anderson, Robert,   Kentucky   Barren County
       Anderson, Robert,   over 16 Male
       Color: Colored
       Anderson, Robert,   over 21 Male
       Color: White
       slave, over 16 Male   **Color:** Colored
Acres of land: 200; Barren Co.; watercourse: Meshacks Creek; Entry: Robt Anderson; Survey: same; Patents: 0; white males over 21: 1; white males 16-21: 0; blacks over 16: 2; total blacks: 5; horses: 4; stud horses: 0; retail stores: 0; tavern license: 0.
Barren County Tax Book, 1800, part 1 - page: 1
FAMILY HISTORY LIBRARY film 7865
Anderson, William,   Kentucky   Barren County
       Anderson, William,   over 21 Male
       Color: White
Acres of land: 200; Barren Co.; watercourse: Boyds Fork; Entry: William Anderson; Survey: same; Patents: 0; white males over 21: 1; white males 16-21: 0; blacks over 16: 0; total blacks: 0; horses: 3; stud horses: 0; retail stores: 0; tavern license: 0.
Barren County Tax Book, 1800, part 1 - page: 1
FAMILY HISTORY LIBRARY film 7865
Anderson, William,   Kentucky   Barren County

Anderson, William,   over 21 Male
Color: White
Anderson, William,   over 16 Male
Color: Colored
Acres of land: 500; Barren Co.; watercourse: Sinks? of Beaver Creek; Entry: John Jerot; Survey: same; Patents: same; white males over 21: 1; white males 16-21: 0; blacks over 16: 1; total blacks: 3; horses: 4; stud horses: 0; retail store: 0; tavern: 0.
Barren County Tax Book, 1800, part 1 - page: 1
FAMILY HISTORY LIBRARY film 7865

Ansel or Alfred, Alfred or Ansel,   Kentucky   Barren County
        Ansel or Alfred, Alfred or Ansel, over 21 Male   **Color:** White
Acres of land: 200; Barren Co.; watercourse: Skeggs Creek; Entry: Ansel Alfred; Survey: same; Patents: 0; white males over 21: 1; white males 16-21: 0; blacks over 16: 0; total blacks: 0; horses: 18; stud horses: 0; retail stores: 0; tavern license: 0.
Barren County Tax Book, 1800, part 1 - page: 1
FAMILY HISTORY LIBRARY film 7865

Austin, Jonas, Kentucky   Barren County
        Austin, Jonas, over 21 Male   **Color:** White
Acres of land: 0; Barren Co.; watercourse: 0; Entry: 0; Survey: 0; Patents: 0; white males over 21: 1; white males 16-21: 0; blacks over 16: 0; total blacks: 0; horses: 0; stud horses: 0; retail stores: 0; tavern license: 0.
Barren County Tax Book, 1800, part 1 - page: 1
FAMILY HISTORY LIBRARY film 7865

Barnet, William,   Kentucky   Barren County
        Barnet, William,   over 21 Male   **Color:** White
Acres of land: 0; County: 0; watercourse: 0; Entry: 0; Survey: 0; Patents: 0; white males over 21: 1; white males 16-21: 0; blacks over 16: 0; total blacks: 0; horses: 1; stud horses: 0; tavern license: 0.
Barren County Tax Book, 1800, part 1 - page: 2
FAMILY HISTORY LIBRARY film 7865

Barnett, Wm, Kentucky   Barren County?
        Barnett, Wm,   Male
The entry for land owned by John Robinson was in his name.
Barren County Tax Book, 1800, part 1 - page: 13
FAMILY HISTORY LIBRARY film 7865

Barten, James,   Kentucky   Barren County
        Barten, James, over 21 Male   **Color:** White
Acres of land: 200; Barren Co.; watercourse: Peters Creek; Entry: James Thomas; Survey: same; Patents: 0; white males over 21: 1; white males 16-21: 0; blacks over 16: 0; total blacks: 0; horses: 3; stud horses: 0; tavern license: 0.
Barren County Tax Book, 1800, part 1 - page: 2
FAMILY HISTORY LIBRARY film 7865

Bates, James, Kentucky   Barren County?
        Bates, James,   Male
The entry for land owned by Thomas Bates was in his name.
Barren County Tax Book, 1800, part 1 - page: 1
FAMILY HISTORY LIBRARY film 7865

Bates, James, Kentucky   Barren County
        Bates, James,   over 21 Male   **Color:** White
Acres of land: 0; Barren Co.; watercourse: 0; Entry: 0; Survey: 0; Patents: 0; white males over 21: 1; white males 16-21: 0; blacks over 16: 0; total blacks: 0; horses: 1; stud horses: 0; retail stores: 0; tavern license: 0.
Barren County Tax Book, 1800, part 1 - page: 1
FAMILY HISTORY LIBRARY film 7865

Bates, Joseph, Jnr   Kentucky   Barren County
        Bates, Joseph, Jnr   over 21 Male   **Color:** White
Acres of land: 200; Barren Co.; watercourse: Green River; Entry: Joseph Bates Jnr; Survey: same; Patents: same; white males over 21: 1; white males 16-21: 0; blacks over 16: 0; total blacks: 0; horses: 1; stud horses: 0; tavern license: 0.
Barren County Tax Book, 1800, part 1 - page: 2
FAMILY HISTORY LIBRARY film 7865

Bates, Joseph, Senr   Kentucky   Barren County
        Bates, Joseph, Senr   over 21 Male   **Color:** White
Acres of land: 200; Barren Co.; watercourse: Green River; Entry: Joseph Bates Senr; Survey: same; Patents: same; white males over 21: 1; white males 16-21: 0; blacks over 16: 0; total blacks: 0; horses: 4; stud horses: 0; tavern license: 0.
Barren County Tax Book, 1800, part 1 - page: 2
FAMILY HISTORY LIBRARY film 7865

Bates, Robt, Kentucky   Barren County?

Bates, Robt,   Male
The entry for land owned by Thomas Bates was in
his name.
Barren County Tax Book, 1800, part 1 - page: 1
FAMILY HISTORY LIBRARY film 7865
Bates, Thomas,   Kentucky   Barren
County
         Bates, Thomas, 16-21   Male   **Color:**
         White
         Bates, Thomas, over 21 Male   **Color:**
         White
Acres of land: 200; Barren Co.; watercourse:
Green River; Entry: James Bates; Survey: same;
Patents: 0; white males over 21: 1; white males 16-
21: 1; blacks over 16: 0; total blacks: 0; horses: 4;
stud horses: 0; retail stores: 0; tavern license: 0.
Barren County Tax Book, 1800, part 1 - page: 1
FAMILY HISTORY LIBRARY film 7865
Bates, Thomas,   Kentucky   Barren
County
         Bates, Thomas, Male
Acres of land: 200; Barren Co.; watercourse:
Green River; Entry: Robt Bates; Survey: same;
Patents: 0; white males over 21: 0; white males 16-
21: 0; blacks over 16: 0; total blacks: 0; horses: 0;
stud horses: 0; retail stores: 0; tavern license: 0.
Barren County Tax Book, 1800, part 1 - page: 1
FAMILY HISTORY LIBRARY film 7865
Bates, Thomas,   Kentucky   Barren
County
         Bates, Thomas, Male
Acres of land: 200; Barren Co.; watercourse:
Green River; Entry: Thos Bates; Survey: same;
Patents: 0; white males over 21: 0; white males 16-
21: 0; blacks over 16: 0; total blacks: 0; horses: 0;
stud horses: 0; retail stores: 0; tavern license: 0.
Barren County Tax Book, 1800, part 1 - page: 1
FAMILY HISTORY LIBRARY film 7865
Beard, Andrew,   Kentucky   Barren
County
         Beard, Andrew,   over 21 Male
         Color: White
         slave, over 16 Male   **Color:** Colored
         slave, over 16 Male   **Color:** Colored
Acres of land: 180; Barren Co.; watercourse: Little
Barren; Entry: Wm Lamb; Survey: same; Patents:
same; white males over 21: 1; white males 16-21:
0; blacks over 16: 2; total blacks: 3; horses: 5; stud
horses: 0; tavern license: 0.

Barren County Tax Book, 1800, part 1 - page: 2
FAMILY HISTORY LIBRARY film 7865
Beard, Andrew,   Kentucky   Barren
County
         Beard, Andrew,   Male
Acres of land: 200; Cumberland Co.; watercourse:
Bear Creek; Entry: Andrew Beard; Survey: same;
Patents: 0; white males over 21: 0; white males 16-
21: 0; blacks over 16: 0; total blacks: 0; horses: 0;
stud horses: 0; tavern license: 0.
Barren County Tax Book, 1800, part 1 - page: 2
FAMILY HISTORY LIBRARY film 7865
Beard, Andrew,   Kentucky   Barren
County
         Beard, Andrew,   Male
Acres of land: 200; Cumberland Co.; watercourse:
Bear Creek; Entry: Andrew Beard; Survey: same;
Patents: 0; white males over 21: 0; white males 16-
21: 0; blacks over 16: 0; total blacks: 0; horses: 0;
stud horses: 0; tavern license: 0.
Barren County Tax Book, 1800, part 1 - page: 2
FAMILY HISTORY LIBRARY film 7865
Beard, Andrew,   Kentucky   Barren
County
         Beard, Andrew,   Male
Acres of land: 200; Green Co.; watercourse:
Crokes; Entry: Andrew Beard; Survey: same;
Patents: same; white males over 21: 0; white males
16-21: 0; blacks over 16: 0; total blacks: 0; horses:
0; stud horses: 0; tavern license: 0.
Barren County Tax Book, 1800, part 1 - page: 2
FAMILY HISTORY LIBRARY film 7865
Belcher, Moses,   Kentucky   Barren
County
         Belcher, Moses,   Male
Acres of land: 200; Barren Co.; watercourse: E. F.
Big Barren; Entry: Moses Belcher; Survey: same;
Patents: 0; white males over 21: 1; white males 16-
21: 0; blacks over 16: 0; total blacks: 0; horses: 3;
stud horses: 0; tavern license: 0.
Barren County Tax Book, 1800, part 1 - page: 2
FAMILY HISTORY LIBRARY film 7865
Bell, Henry,   Kentucky   Barren County
         Bell, Henry,   over 21 Male   **Color:**
         White
Acres of land: 110; Barren Co.; watercourse:
Green River; Entry: Henry Bell; Survey: same;
Patents: 0; white males over 21: 1; white males 16-
21: 0; blacks over 16: 0; total blacks: 0; horses: 3;
stud horses: 0; tavern license: 0.

Barren County Tax Book, 1800, part 1 - page: 2
FAMILY HISTORY LIBRARY film 7865
Bell, William, Kentucky   Barren County
        Bell, William,   over 21 Male   **Color:**
        White
Acres of land: 140; Barren Co.; watercourse:
Beaver Creek; Entry: Wm Bell; Survey: same;
Patents: 0; white males over 21: 1; white males 16-
21: 0; blacks over 16: 0; total blacks: 0; horses: 2;
stud horses: 0; tavern license: 0.
Barren County Tax Book, 1800, part 1 - page: 2
FAMILY HISTORY LIBRARY film 7865
Bell, William, Kentucky   Barren County
        Bell, William,   over 21 Male   **Color:**
        White
        slave,   over 16 Male   **Color:** Colored
Acres of land: 120; Barren Co.; watercourse:
Green River; Entry: Wm Bell; Survey: same;
Patents: 0; white males over 21: 1; white males 16-
21: 0; blacks over 16: 1; total blacks: 1; horses: 2;
stud horses: 0; tavern license: 0.
Barren County Tax Book, 1800, part 1 - page: 2
FAMILY HISTORY LIBRARY film 7865
Bell, William, Kentucky   Barren County
        Bell, William,   Male
Acres of land: 145; Jessamine Co.; watercourse:
Kentucky River; Entry: 0; Survey: 0; Patents: 0;
white males over 21: 0; white males 16-21: 0;
blacks over 16: 0; total blacks: 0; horses: 0; stud
horses: 0; tavern license: 0.
Barren County Tax Book, 1800, part 1 - page: 2
FAMILY HISTORY LIBRARY film 7865
Bennit, John, Kentucky   Barren County
        Bennit, John,   over 21 Male   **Color:**
        White
        Bennit, 16-21   Male   **Color:** White
Acres of land: 0; Barren Co.; watercourse: 0;
Entry: 0; Survey: 0; Patents: 0; white males over
21: 1; white males 16-21: 1; blacks over 16: 0;
total blacks: 2; horses: 5; stud horses: 0; retail
stores: 0; tavern license: 0.
Barren County Tax Book, 1800, part 1 - page: 1
FAMILY HISTORY LIBRARY film 7865
Bennit, Stephen,   Kentucky   Barren
County
        Bennit, Stephen,   over 21 Male
        Color: White
Acres of land: 200; Barren Co.; watercourse:
Beaver Creek; Entry: Stephen Bennit; Survey:
same; Patents: 0; white males over 21: 1; white

males 16-21: 0; blacks over 16: 0; total blacks: 0;
horses: 7; stud horses: 0; retail stores: 0; tavern
license: 0.
Barren County Tax Book, 1800, part 1 - page: 1
FAMILY HISTORY LIBRARY film 7865
Bennit, William, Senr Kentucky   Barren
County
        Bennit, William, Senr   over 21 Male
        Color: White
Acres of land: 100; Barren Co.; watercourse:
Fallen Timber; Entry: Wm Bennit; Survey: 0;
Patents: 0; white males over 21: 1; white males 16-
21: 0; blacks over 16: 0; total blacks: 1; horses: 3;
stud horses: 0; tavern license: 0.
Barren County Tax Book, 1800, part 1 - page: 2
FAMILY HISTORY LIBRARY film 7865
Berks, John, Jnr   Kentucky   Barren
County
        Berks, John, Jnr over 21 Male   **Color:**
        White
Acres of land: 0; Barren Co.; watercourse: 0;
Entry: 0; Survey: 0; Patents: 0; white males over
21: 1; white males 16-21: 0; blacks over 16: 0;
total blacks: 0; horses: 1; stud horses: 0; retail
stores: 0; tavern license: 0.
Barren County Tax Book, 1800, part 1 - page: 1
FAMILY HISTORY LIBRARY film 7865
Berks, John, Senr   Kentucky   Barren
County
        Berks, John, Senr   over 21 Male
        Color: White
Acres of land: 200; Barren Co; watercourse:
Bluespring Creek; Entry: Martin Frayser?; Survey:
same; Patents: same; white males over 21: 1; white
males 16-21: 0; blacks over 16: 0; total blacks: 0;
horses: 3; stud horses: 0; retailstore: 0; tavern lic.:
1.
Barren County Tax Book, 1800, part 1 - page: 1
FAMILY HISTORY LIBRARY film 7865
Bernsides, Robt,   Kentucky   Barren
County?
        Bernsides, Robt,   Male
The entry for land owned by James Johnson was in
his name.
Barren County Tax Book, 1800, part 1 - page: 9
FAMILY HISTORY LIBRARY film 7865
Bernsides, Walter,   Kentucky   Barren
County?
        Bernsides, Walter,   Male

The entry for land owned by Hugh Marshall was in his name.
Barren County Tax Book, 1800, part 1 - page: 11
FAMILY HISTORY LIBRARY film 7865
Bishong, Henry, Kentucky Barren County
      Bishong, Henry, over 21 Male
      Color: White
Acres of land: 200; Barren Co.; watercourse: E. F. Big Barren; Entry: Henry Bishong; Survey: Henry Bishong; Patents: 0; white males over 21: 1; white males 16-21: 0; blacks over 16: 0; total blacks: 0; horses: 5; stud horses: 0; tavern license: 0.
Barren County Tax Book, 1800, part 1 - page: 2
FAMILY HISTORY LIBRARY film 7865
Bishop, William, Kentucky Barren County
      Bishop, William, 16-21 Male
      Color: White
      Bishop, William, over 21 Male
      Color: White
      slave, over 16 Male **Color:** Colored
      slave, over 16 Male **Color:** Colored
      slave, over 16 Male **Color:** Colored
Acres of land: 200; Barren Co.; watercourse: Bluespring Creek; Entry: Wm Bishop; Survey: same; Patents: 0; white males over 21: 1; white males 16-21: 1; blacks over 16: 3; total blacks: 5; horses: 3; stud horses: 0; retail stores: 0; tavern license: 0.
Barren County Tax Book, 1800, part 1 - page: 1
FAMILY HISTORY LIBRARY film 7865
Bishop, William, Kentucky Barren County
      Bishop, William, Male
Acres of land: 200; Barren Co.; watercourse: Bluespring Creek; Entry: Lowry Bishop; Survey: same; Patents: 0; white males over 21: 0; white males 16-21: 0; blacks over 16: 0; total blacks: 0; horses: 0; stud horses: 0; retail stores: 0; tavern license: 0.
Barren County Tax Book, 1800, part 1 - page: 1
FAMILY HISTORY LIBRARY film 7865
Black, James, Kentucky Barren County
      Black, James, over 21 Male **Color:** White
      Black, over 21 Male **Color:** White
      Black, over 21 Male **Color:** White
Acres of land: 200; Barren Co.; watercourse: Bluespring Creek; Entry: James Black; Survey:

same; Patents: 0; white males over 21: 3; white males 16-21: 0; blacks over 16: 0; total blacks: 0; horses: 6; stud horses: 0; retail stores: 0; tavern license: 0.
Barren County Tax Book, 1800, part 1 - page: 1
FAMILY HISTORY LIBRARY film 7865
Black, Robert, Kentucky Barren County
      Black, Robert, Male
Acres of land: 150; Barren Co.; watercourse: 0; Entry: Robt Black; Survey: 0; Patents: 0; white males over 21: 0; white males 16-21: 0; blacks over 16: 0; total blacks: 0; horses: 0; stud horses: 0; retail stores: 0; tavern license: 0.
Barren County Tax Book, 1800, part 1 - page: 1
FAMILY HISTORY LIBRARY film 7865
Blakeley, Littleberry, Kentucky Barren County
      Blakeley, Littleberry, 16-21 Male
      Color: White
Acres of land: 0; County: 0, watercourse: 0; Entry: 0; Survey: 0; Patents: 0; white males over 21: 0; white males 16-21: 1; blacks over 16: 0; total blacks: 0; horses: 1; stud horses: 0; tavern license: 0.
Barren County Tax Book, 1800, part 1 - page: 2
FAMILY HISTORY LIBRARY film 7865
Blakey, Thomas, Kentucky Barren County
      Blakey, Thomas, over 21 Male
      Color: White
Acres of land: 0; County: 0; watercourse: 0; Entry: 0; Survey: 0; Patents: 0; white males over 21: 1; white males 16-21: 0; blacks over 16: 0; total blacks: 0; horses: 1; stud horses: 0; tavern license: 0.
Barren County Tax Book, 1800, part 1 - page: 2
FAMILY HISTORY LIBRARY film 7865
Blakey, William, Kentucky Barren County
      Blakey, William, Male
Acres of land: 200; Barren Co.; watercourse: Beaver Creek; Entry: Wm Blakey; Survey: same; Patents: 0; white males over 21: 0; white males 16-21: 0; blacks over 16: 0; total blacks: 0; horses: 0; stud horses: 0; retail stores: 0; tavern license: 0.
Barren County Tax Book, 1800, part 1 - page: 1
FAMILY HISTORY LIBRARY film 7865
Blakey, William, Kentucky Barren County

Blakey, William,   over 21 Male
Color: White
Blakey, William,   over 16 Male
Color: Colored
    slave, over 16 Male   **Color:** Colored
    slave, over 16 Male   **Color:** Colored
    slave, over 16 Male   **Color:** Colored
Acres of land: 600; Barren Co.; watercourse: Sinks of Beaver Creek; Entry: B Sheppord assee of J M Sheppord; Survey: same; Patents: same; white males over 21: 1; white males 16-21: 0; blacks over 16: 4; total blacks: 7; horses: 3.
Barren County Tax Book, 1800, part 1 - page: 1
FAMILY HISTORY LIBRARY film 7865
Blakman, Adam,   Kentucky   Barren County
        Blakman, Adam,   over 21 Male
        Color: White
Acres of land: 0; County: 0; watercourse: 0; Entry: 0; Survey: 0; Patents: 0; white males over 21: 1; white males 16-21: 0; blacks over 16: 0; total blacks: 0; horses: 0; stud horses: 0; retail stores: 0; tavern license: 0.
Barren County Tax Book, 1800, part 1 - page: 3
FAMILY HISTORY LIBRARY film 7865
Blasrave, Harrison,   Kentucky   Barren County
        Blasrave, Harrison,   over 21 Male
        Color: White
Acres of land: 0; County: 0; watercourse: 0; Entry: 0; Survey: 0; Patents: 0; white males over 21: 1; white males 16-21: 0; blacks over 16: 0; total blacks: 1; horses: 2?; stud horses: 0; tavern license: 0.
Barren County Tax Book, 1800, part 1 - page: 2
FAMILY HISTORY LIBRARY film 7865
Bogard, Jacob,   Kentucky   Barren County
        Bogard, Jacob, over 21 Male   **Color:** White
Acres of land: 0; Barren Co.; watercourse: 0; Entry: 0; Survey: 0; Patents: 0; white males over 21: 1; white males 16-21: 0; blacks over 16: 0; total blacks: 0; horses: 6; stud horses: 0; retail stores: 0; tavern license: 0.
Barren County Tax Book, 1800, part 1 - page: 1
FAMILY HISTORY LIBRARY film 7865
Bourne, Abner,   Kentucky   Barren County

Bourne, Abner, over 16 Male   **Color:** Colored
Bourne, Abner, over 21 Male   **Color:** White
    slave, over 16 Male   **Color:** Colored
Acres of land: 166; Barren Co.; watercourse: South Fork of Beaver Creek; Entry: Scott; Survey: Scott; Patents: Scott; white males over 21: 1; white males 16-21: 0; blacks over 16: 2; total blacks: 4; horses: 0; stud horses: 0; tavern.: 0.
Barren County Tax Book, 1800, part 1 - page: 1
FAMILY HISTORY LIBRARY film 7865
Boyd, John,   Kentucky   Barren County
        Boyd, John,   over 21 Male   **Color:** White
Acres of land: 200; Barren Co.; watercourse: Peters Creek; Entry: Josiah McKenny; Survey: John Boyd; Patents: 0; white males over 21: 1; white males 16-21: 0; blacks over 16: 0; total blacks: 0; horses: 2; stud horses: 0; retail stores: 0; tavern: 0.
Barren County Tax Book, 1800, part 1 - page: 3
FAMILY HISTORY LIBRARY film 7865
Breed, Avery, Kentucky   Barren County
        Breed, Avery,   over 21 Male   **Color:** White
Acres of land: 200; Barren Co.; watercourse: E. F. Big Barren; Entry: Avery Breed; Survey: same; Patents: 0; white males over 21: 1; white males 16-21: 0; blacks over 16: 0; total blacks: 1; horses: 4; stud horses: 0; tavern license: 0.
Barren County Tax Book, 1800, part 1 - page: 2
FAMILY HISTORY LIBRARY film 7865
Breed, Nathan,   Kentucky   Barren County
        Breed, Nathan, over 21 Male   **Color:** White
Acres of land: 200; Barren Co.; watercourse: Mill Creek; Entry: Nathan Breed; Survey: same; Patents: 0; white males over 21: 1; white males 16-21: 0; blacks over 16: 0; total blacks: 2; horses: 7; stud horses: 0; tavern license: 0.
Barren County Tax Book, 1800, part 1 - page: 2
FAMILY HISTORY LIBRARY film 7865
Breed, Nathan,   Kentucky   Barren County
        Breed, Nathan, Male
Acres of land: 191; Barren Co.; watercourse: Mill Creek; Entry: Wm Hunter; Survey: same; Patents: 0; white males over 21: 0; white males 16-21: 0;

blacks over 16: 0; total blacks: 0; horses: 0; stud horses: 0; tavern license: 0.
Barren County Tax Book, 1800, part 1 - page: 2
FAMILY HISTORY LIBRARY film 7865
Breed, Nathan,   Kentucky   Barren County
     Breed, Nathan,   Male
Acres of land: 100; Barren Co.; watercourse: Mill Creek; Entry: Wm M Layne?; Survey: same; Patents: 0; white males over 21: 0; white males 16-21: 0; blacks over 16: 0; total blacks: 0; horses: 0; stud horses: 0; tavern license: 0.
Barren County Tax Book, 1800, part 1 - page: 2
FAMILY HISTORY LIBRARY film 7865
Brough, Robt, Kentucky   Barren County?
     Brough, Robt,   Male
The entry for land owned by Edmond Rogers was in his name.
Barren County Tax Book, 1800, part 1 - page: 13
FAMILY HISTORY LIBRARY film 7865
Brown, William,   Kentucky   Barren County
     Brown, William,   over 21 Male   **Color:** White
Acres of land: 0; County: 0; watercourse: 0; Entry: 0; Survey: 0; Patents: 0; white males over 21: 1; white males 16-21: 0; blacks over 16: 0; total blacks: 0; horses: 1; stud horses: 0; tavern license: 0.
Barren County Tax Book, 1800, part 1 - page: 2
FAMILY HISTORY LIBRARY film 7865
Bureham, Dennaige,   Kentucky   Barren County
     Bureham, Dennaige,   over 21 Male   **Color:** White
Acres of land: 0; County: 0; watercourse: 0; Entry: 0; Survey: 0; Patents: 0; white males over 21: 1; white males 16-21: 0; blacks over 16: 0; total blacks: 0; horses: 3; stud horses: 0; tavern license: 0.
Barren County Tax Book, 1800, part 1 - page: 2
FAMILY HISTORY LIBRARY film 7865
Bybee, Allen,   Kentucky   Barren County
     Bybee, Allen,   over 21 Male   **Color:** White
Acres of land: 100; Barren Co.; watercourse: Nobob; Entry: Joseph Dennis; Survey: same; Patents: 0; white males over 21: 1; white males 16-21: 0; blacks over 16: 0; total blacks: 0; horses: 1; stud horses: 0; tavern license: 0.

Barren County Tax Book, 1800, part 1 - page: 2
FAMILY HISTORY LIBRARY film 7865
Bybee, John,   Kentucky   Barren County
     Bybee, John,   over 21 Male   **Color:** White
Acres of land: 200; Barren Co.; watercourse: Nobob; Entry: John Bybee; Survey: same; Patents: 0; white males over 21: 1; white males 16-21: 0; blacks over 16: 0; total blacks: 0; horses: 3; stud horses: 0; tavern license: 0.
Barren County Tax Book, 1800, part 1 - page: 2
FAMILY HISTORY LIBRARY film 7865
Bybee, John,   Kentucky   Barren County
     Bybee, John,   over 21 Male   **Color:** White
     Bybee,   over 21 Male   **Color:** White
     Bybee,   16-21   Male   **Color:** White
Acres of land: 200; Barren Co.; watercourse: Beaver Creek; Entry: John Bybee; Survey: same; Patents: 0; white males over 21: 2; white males 16-21: 1; blacks over 16: 0; total blacks: 0; horses: 5; stud horses: 0; tavern license: 0.
Barren County Tax Book, 1800, part 1 - page: 2
FAMILY HISTORY LIBRARY film 7865
Bybee, Nile McCan,   Kentucky   Barren County
     Bybee, Nile McCan,   over 21 Male   **Color:** White
Acres of land: 0; Barren Co.; watercourse: 0; Entry: 0; Survey: 0; Patents: 0; white males over 21: 1; white males 16-21: 0; blacks over 16: 0; total blacks: 0; horses: 3; stud horses: 0; retail stores: 0; tavern license: 0.
Barren County Tax Book, 1800, part 1 - page: 1
FAMILY HISTORY LIBRARY film 7865
Byers, James, Kentucky   Barren County
     Byers, James,   over 21 Male   **Color:** White
Acres of land: 0; Barren Co.; watercourse: 0; Entry: 0; Survey: 0; Patents: 0; white males over 21: 1; white males 16-21: 0; blacks over 16: 0; total blacks: 0; horses: 0; stud horses: 0; retail stores: 0; tavern license: 0.
Barren County Tax Book, 1800, part 1 - page: 3
FAMILY HISTORY LIBRARY film 7865
Byram, Lewis, Kentucky   Barren County
     Byram, Lewis,   over 21 Male   **Color:** White
Acres of land: 75; Barren Co.; watercourse: L. Barren; Entry: Surtey; Survey: same; Patents: 0;

white males over 21: 1; white males 16-21: 0; blacks over 16: 0; total blacks: 1; horses: 3; stud horses: 1; retail stores: 0; tavern license: 0.
Barren County Tax Book, 1800, part 1 - page: 3
FAMILY HISTORY LIBRARY film 7865
Cammel, Wm, Kentucky Barren County?
Cammel, Wm, Male
The entry for land owned by William Martin was in his name.
Barren County Tax Book, 1800, part 1 - page: 11
FAMILY HISTORY LIBRARY film 7865
Campbell, Michael, Kentucky Barren County?
Campbell, Michael, Male
The entry for land owned by John Flint was in his name.
Barren County Tax Book, 1800, part 1 - page: 6
FAMILY HISTORY LIBRARY film 7865
Carlile, Thomas, Kentucky Barren County
Carlile, Thomas, over 21 Male
Color: White
Acres of land: 0; County: 0; watercourse: 0; Entry: 0; Survey: 0; Patents: 0; white males over 21: 1; white males 16-21: 0; blacks over 16: 0; total blacks: 0; horses: 1; stud horses: 0; retail stores: 0; tavern license: 0.
Barren County Tax Book, 1800, part 1 - page: 3
FAMILY HISTORY LIBRARY film 7865
Carr?, Nathan, Kentucky Barren County
Carr?, Nathan, over 21 Male **Color:** White
Acres of land: 0; County: 0; watercourse: 0; Entry: 0; Survey: 0; Patents: 0; white males over 21: 1; white males 16-21: 0; blacks over 16: 0; total blacks: 0; horses: 1; stud horses: 0; retail stores: 0; tavern license: 0.
Barren County Tax Book, 1800, part 1 - page: 3
FAMILY HISTORY LIBRARY film 7865
Carrick, John Montgomery, Kentucky Barren County
Carrick, John Montgomery, over 21 Male **Color:** White
Acres of land: 0; County: 0; watercourse: 0; Entry: 0; Survey: 0; Patent: 0; white males over 21: 1; white males 16-21: 0; blacks over 16: 0; total blacks: 0; horses: 1; stud horses: 0; tavern license: 0.

Barren County Tax Book, 1800, part 1 - page: 4
FAMILY HISTORY LIBRARY film 7865
Carrick, Moses, Kentucky Barren County
Carrick, Moses, over 21 Male
Color: White
Acres of land: 0; County: 0; watercourse: 0; Entry: 0; Survey: 0; Patent: 0; white males over 21: 1; white males 16-21: 0; blacks over 16: 0; total blacks: 0; horses: 1; stud horses: 0; tavern license: 0.
Barren County Tax Book, 1800, part 1 - page: 4
FAMILY HISTORY LIBRARY film 7865
Carrolson?, Kentucky Barren County?
Carrolson?, Male
The patent for land owned by William Martin was in his name.
Barren County Tax Book, 1800, part 1 - page: 11
FAMILY HISTORY LIBRARY film 7865
Carter, Daniel, Kentucky Barren County
Carter, Daniel, over 21 Male **Color:** White
slave, over 16 Male **Color:** Colored
slave, over 16 Male **Color:** Colored
slave, over 16 Male **Color:** Colored
slave, over 16 Male **Color:** Colored
Acres of land: 150; Barren Co.; watercourse: Green River; Entry: 0; Survey: 0; Patents: 0; white males over 21: 1; white males 16-21: 0; blacks over 16: 4; total blacks: 8; horses: 5; stud horses: 0; retail stores: 0; tavern license: 0.
Barren County Tax Book, 1800, part 1 - page: 3
FAMILY HISTORY LIBRARY film 7865
Carter, Daniel, Kentucky Barren County
Carter, Daniel, Male
Acres of land: 30; Barren Co.; watercourse: Green River; Entry: Jesse Clarke; Survey: same; Patents: same; white males over 21: 0; white males 16-21: 0; blacks over 16: 0; total blacks: 0; horses: 0; stud horses: 0; retail stores: 0; tavern license: 0.
Barren County Tax Book, 1800, part 1 - page: 3
FAMILY HISTORY LIBRARY film 7865
Carter, Daniel, Kentucky Barren County
Carter, Daniel, Male
Acres of land: 150; Barren Co.; watercourse: Green River; Entry: Roberts; Survey: same; Patents: 0; white males over 21: 0; white males 16-

21: 0; blacks over 16: 0; total blacks: 0; horses: 0; stud horses: 0; retail stores: 0; tavern license: 0.
Barren County Tax Book, 1800, part 1 - page: 3
FAMILY HISTORY LIBRARY film 7865
Carter, James, Kentucky Barren County
Carter, James, over 21 Male **Color:** White
Acres of land: 0; County: 0; watercourse: 0; Entry: 0; Survey: 0; Patents: 0; white males over 21: 1; white males 16-21: 0; blacks over 16: 0; total blacks: 0; horses: 3; stud horses: 0; tavern license: 0.
Barren County Tax Book, 1800, part 1 - page: 4
FAMILY HISTORY LIBRARY film 7865
Carter, James, Kentucky Barren County
Carter, James, over 21 Male **Color:** White
Acres of land: 200; Barren Co.; watercourse: E. F. Big Barren; Entry: James Carter; Survey: same; Patent: 0; white males over 21: 1; white males 16-21: 0; blacks over 16: 0; total blacks: 1; horses: 2; stud horses: 0; tavern license: 0.
Barren County Tax Book, 1800, part 1 - page: 4
FAMILY HISTORY LIBRARY film 7865
Carter, William, Kentucky Barren County
Carter, William, over 21 Male **Color:** White
Acres of land: 0; County: 0; watercourse: 0; Entry: 0; Survey: 0; Patents: 0; white males over 21: 1; white males 16-21: 0; blacks over 16: 0; total blacks: 0; horses: 2; stud horses: 0; tavern license: 0.
Barren County Tax Book, 1800, part 1 - page: 4
FAMILY HISTORY LIBRARY film 7865
Chaplin, Abrhm, Kentucky Barren County?
Chaplin, Abrhm, Male
The entry for land owned by William Renick was in his name.
Barren County Tax Book, 1800, part 1 - page: 12
FAMILY HISTORY LIBRARY film 7865
Chaplin, Abrm, Kentucky Barren County?
Chaplin, Abrm, Male
The entry for land owned by Henry Renick was in his name.

Barren County Tax Book, 1800, part 1 - page: 12
FAMILY HISTORY LIBRARY film 7865
Chapline, A, Kentucky Barren County?
Chapline, A, Male
The patent for land owned by Edmond Rogers was in the names of E Rogers & A Chapline.
Barren County Tax Book, 1800, part 1 - page: 13
FAMILY HISTORY LIBRARY film 7865
Chisum, George, Kentucky Barren County
Chisum, George, over 21 Male **Color:** White
Acres of land: 200; Barren Co.; watercourse: Mill Creek; Entry: George Chisum; Survey: same; Patent: 0; white males over 21: 1; white males 16-21: 0; blacks over 16: 0; total blacks: 0; horses: 2; stud horses: 0; tavern license: 0.
Barren County Tax Book, 1800, part 1 - page: 4
FAMILY HISTORY LIBRARY film 7865
Chisum, John, Kentucky Barren County
Chisum, John, over 21 Male **Color:** White
slave, over 16 Male **Color:** Colored
Acres of land: 200; Barren Co.; watercourse: Mill Creek; Entry: John Chisum; Survey: same; Patent: 0; white males over 21: 1; white males 16-21: 0; blacks over 16: 1; total blacks: 1; horses: 4; stud horses: 0; tavern license: 0.
Barren County Tax Book, 1800, part 1 - page: 4
FAMILY HISTORY LIBRARY film 7865
Cincade [Kincade], Joseph, Kentucky Barren County
Cincade [Kincade], Joseph, over 21 Male **Color:** White
Acres of land: 39; Barren Co.; watercourse: E F Big Barren; Entry: Joseph Cincade; Survey: 0; Patent: 0; white males over 21: 1; white males 16-21: 0; blacks over 16: 0; total blacks: 0; horses: 1; stud horses: 0; tavern license: 0.
Barren County Tax Book, 1800, part 1 - page: 4
FAMILY HISTORY LIBRARY film 7865
Clarke, Geo R., Kentucky Barren County?
Clarke, Geo R., Male
The entry for land owned by Edmond Rogers was in his name.
Barren County Tax Book, 1800, part 1 - page: 13
FAMILY HISTORY LIBRARY film 7865
Clarke, Jacob, Kentucky Barren County
Clarke, Jacob, Male

Acres of land: 58 1/2; Barren Co.; watercourse: S. F. Little Barren; Entry: Brian Trent; Survey: same; Patents: 0; white males over 21: 0; white males 16-21: 0; blacks over 16: 0; total blacks: 0; horses: 0; stud horses: 0; retail stores: 0; tavern: 0.
Barren County Tax Book, 1800, part 1 - page: 3
FAMILY HISTORY LIBRARY film 7865

Clarke, Jacob, Kentucky   Barren County
  Clarke, Jacob, over 21 Male   **Color:** White
Acres of land: 150; Barren Co.; watercourse: 0; Entry: Andrew Walker; Survey: same; Patents: same; white males over 21: 1; white males 16-21: 0; blacks over 16: 0; total blacks: 0; horses: 2; stud horses: 0; retail stores: 0; tavern license: 0.
Barren County Tax Book, 1800, part 1 - page: 3
FAMILY HISTORY LIBRARY film 7865

Clarke, Jesse, Kentucky   Barren County?
  Clarke, Jesse,   Male
The entry for land owned by Daniel Carter was in his name.
Barren County Tax Book, 1800, part 1 - page: 3
FAMILY HISTORY LIBRARY film 7865

Clarke, Reubin,   Kentucky   Barren County
  Clarke, Reubin,   over 21 Male   **Color:** White
Acres of land: 0; County: 0; watercourse: 0; Entry: 0; Survey: 0; Patents: 0; white males over 21: 1; white males 16-21: 0; blacks over 16: 0; total blacks: 0; horses: 3; stud horses: 0; retail stores: 0; tavern license: 0.
Barren County Tax Book, 1800, part 1 - page: 3
FAMILY HISTORY LIBRARY film 7865

Clarke, Richard,   Kentucky   Barren County?
  Clarke, Richard,   Male
The entry for land owned by Nathaniel Roundtree was in his name.
Barren County Tax Book, 1800, part 1 - page: 12
FAMILY HISTORY LIBRARY film 7865

Clarke, Richard,   Kentucky   Barren County?
  Clarke, Richard,   Male
The entry for land owned by Dudley Roundtree Jun was in his name.
Barren County Tax Book, 1800, part 1 - page: 12
FAMILY HISTORY LIBRARY film 7865

Clarke, Richard,   Kentucky   Barren County?
  Clarke, Richard,   Male
The entry for land owned by Dudley Roundtree senr was in his name.
Barren County Tax Book, 1800, part 1 - page: 12
FAMILY HISTORY LIBRARY film 7865

Clarke, Wilson Ben, Kentucky   Barren County
  Clarke, Wilson Ben,   Male
Acres of land: 1000; Green Co.; watercourse: Russels Creek; Entry: Wm Clarke; Survey: same; Patents: same; white males over 21: 0; white males 16-21: 0; blacks over 16: 0; total blacks: 0; horses: 0; stud horses: 0; tavern license: 0.
Barren County Tax Book, 1800, part 1 - page: 4
FAMILY HISTORY LIBRARY film 7865

Clarke, Wilson Ben, Kentucky   Barren County
  Clarke, Wilson Ben,   Male
Acres of land: 70; Barren Co.; watercourse: S. F. Little Barren; Entry: Wm Clarke; Survey: same; Patents: same; white males over 21: 0; white males 16-21: 0; blacks over 16: 0; total blacks: 0; horses: 0; stud horses: 0; tavern license: 0.
Barren County Tax Book, 1800, part 1 - page: 4
FAMILY HISTORY LIBRARY film 7865

Clarke, Wilson Ben, Kentucky   Barren County
  Clarke, Wilson Ben,   over 21 Male   **Color:** White
  Clarke, 16-21   Male   **Color:** White
  Clarke, 16-21   Male   **Color:** White
  Clarke, 16-21   Male   **Color:** White
  slave, over 16 Male   **Color:** Colored
Acres of land: 930; Barren Co.; watercourse: S. F. Little Barren; Entry: Wm Clarke; Survey: same; Patents: same; white males over 21: 1; white males 16-21: 3; blacks over 16: 1; total blacks: 3; horses: 2; stud horses: 0; tavern license: 0.
Barren County Tax Book, 1800, part 1 - page: 4
FAMILY HISTORY LIBRARY film 7865

Clarke, Wm, Kentucky   Barren County?
  Clarke, Wm,   Male
The entry for land owned by Wilson Ben Clarke was in his name.
Barren County Tax Book, 1800, part 1 - page: 4
FAMILY HISTORY LIBRARY film 7865

Clement, Andrew,   Kentucky   Barren County
  Clement, Andrew,   over 21 Male   **Color:** White

Acres of land: 200; Barren Co.; watercourse: Mill Creek; Entry: Andrew Clement; Survey: same; Patent: 0; white males over 21: 1; white males 16-21: 0; blacks over 16: 0; total blacks: 0; horses: 1; stud horses: 0; tavern license: 0.
Barren County Tax Book, 1800, part 1 - page: 4
FAMILY HISTORY LIBRARY film 7865
Clendennan, Isaac, Kentucky Barren County
Clendennan, Isaac, over 21 Male **Color:** White
Acres of land: 0; County: 0; watercourse: 0; Entry: 0; Survey: 0; Patents: 0; white males over 21: 1; white males 16-21: 0; blacks over 16: 0; total blacks: 0; horses: 2; stud horses: 0; retail stores: 0; tavern license: 0.
Barren County Tax Book, 1800, part 1 - page: 3
FAMILY HISTORY LIBRARY film 7865
Clendennon, Adam, Kentucky Barren County
Clendennon, Adam, over 21 Male **Color:** White
Acres of land: 200; Barren Co.; watercourse: S. F. Little Barren; Entry: Adam Clendennon; Survey: same; Patents: 0; white males over 21: 1; white males 16-21: 0; blacks over 16: 0; total blacks: 2; horses: 2; stud horses: 0; retail store: 0; tavern: 0.
Barren County Tax Book, 1800, part 1 - page: 3
FAMILY HISTORY LIBRARY film 7865
Cochran, Andrew, Kentucky Barren County
Cochran, Andrew, over 21 Male **Color:** White
slave, over 16 Male **Color:** Colored
slave, over 16 Male **Color:** Colored
Acres of land: 200; Barren Co.; watercourse: Swearingans Fork; Entry: Andrew Cochran; Survey: same; Patents: 0; white males over 21: 1; white males 16-21: 0; blacks over 16: 2; total blacks: 4; horses: 3; stud horses: 0; tavern license: 0.
Barren County Tax Book, 1800, part 1 - page: 4
FAMILY HISTORY LIBRARY film 7865
Cockran, William, Kentucky Barren County
Cockran, William, over 21 Male **Color:** White
Acres of land: 0; County: 0; watercourse: 0; Entry: 0; Survey: 0; Patents: 0; white males over 21: 1; white males 16-21: 0; blacks over 16: 0; total

blacks: 0; horses: 1; stud horses: 0; tavern license: 0.
Barren County Tax Book, 1800, part 1 - page: 4
FAMILY HISTORY LIBRARY film 7865
Cole, James, Kentucky Barren County
Cole, James, over 21 Male **Color:** White
Acres of land: 0; County: 0, watercourse: 0; Entry: 0; Survey: 0; Patent: 0; white males over 21: 1; white males 16-21: 0; blacks over 16: 0; total blacks: 0; horses: 3; stud horses: 0; tavern license: 0.
Barren County Tax Book, 1800, part 1 - page: 4
FAMILY HISTORY LIBRARY film 7865
Cole, Stephen, Kentucky Barren County
Cole, Stephen, over 21 Male **Color:** White
slave, over 16 Male **Color:** Colored
Acres of land: 200; Barren Co.; watercourse: Marrowbone; Entry: Stephen Cole; Survey: same; Patents: 0; white males over 21: 1; white males 16-21: 0; blacks over 16: 1; total blacks: 1; horses: 4; stud horses: 0; tavern license: 0.
Barren County Tax Book, 1800, part 1 - page: 4
FAMILY HISTORY LIBRARY film 7865
Cole, William, Kentucky Barren County
Cole, William, over 21 Male **Color:** White
Cole, 16-21 Male **Color:** White
Acres of land: 194; Barren Co.; watercourse: Coles Creek; Entry: Wm Cole; Survey: same; Patent: 0; white males over 21: 1; white males 16-21: 1; blacks over 16: 0; total blacks: 0; horses: 2; stud horses: 0; tavern license: 0.
Barren County Tax Book, 1800, part 1 - page: 4
FAMILY HISTORY LIBRARY film 7865
Conyers, David, Kentucky Barren County
Conyers, David, over 21 Male **Color:** White
Conyers, 16-21 Male **Color:** White
Conyers, 16-21 Male **Color:** White
Acres of land: 200; Barren Co.; watercourse: 0; Entry: David Conyers; Survey: same; Patents: 0; white males over 21: 1; white males 16-21: 2; blacks over 16: 0; total blacks: 0; horses: 3; stud horses: 0; retail stores: 0; tavern license: 0.

Barren County Tax Book, 1800, part 1 - page: 3
FAMILY HISTORY LIBRARY film 7865
Cook, Henry, Kentucky   Barren County
        Cook, Henry,   over 21 Male   **Color:**
        White
Acres of land: 200; Barren Co.; watercourse: Long
Branch; Entry: Henry Cook; Survey: same;
Patents: 0; white males over 21: 1; white males 16-
21: 0; blacks over 16: 0; total blacks: 2; horses: 7;
stud horses: 0; retail stores: 0; tavern license: 0.
Barren County Tax Book, 1800, part 1 - page: 3
FAMILY HISTORY LIBRARY film 7865
Cook, Henry, Kentucky   Barren County
        Cook, Henry,   Male
Acres of land: 150; Barren Co.; watercourse: S
fork of L Barren; Entry: Robt Forbes; Survey:
same; Patents: 0; white males over 21: 0; white
males 16-21: 0; blacks over 16: 0; total blacks: 0;
horses: 0; stud horses: 0; retail stores: 0; tavern: 0.
Barren County Tax Book, 1800, part 1 - page: 3
FAMILY HISTORY LIBRARY film 7865
Cook, Henry, Kentucky   Barren County
        Cook, Henry,   Male
Acres of land: 100; Barren Co.; watercourse: Long
Branch; Entry: James Forbes; Survey: same;
Patents: 0; white males over 21: 0; white males 16-
21: 0; blacks over 16: 0; total blacks: 0; horses: 0;
stud horses: 0; retail stores: 0; tavern license: 0.
Barren County Tax Book, 1800, part 1 - page: 3
FAMILY HISTORY LIBRARY film 7865
Cook, Henry, Kentucky   Barren County
        Cook, Henry,   Male
Acres of land: 200; Barren Co.; watercourse: Long
Branch; Entry: Henry Skeggs; Survey: same;
Patents: 0; white males over 21: 0; white males 16-
21: 0; blacks over 16: 0; total blacks: 0; horses: 0;
stud horses: 0; retail stores: 0; tavern license: 0.
Barren County Tax Book, 1800, part 1 - page: 3
FAMILY HISTORY LIBRARY film 7865
Cotney, Sarah, Kentucky   Barren
County?
        Cotney, Sarah, Female
The entry for land owned by John Defevers was in
her name.
Barren County Tax Book, 1800, part 1 - page: 5
FAMILY HISTORY LIBRARY film 7865
Courts, John, Kentucky   Barren County
        Courts, John,   over 21 Male   **Color:**
        White
        slave, over 16 Male   **Color:** Colored

Acres of land: 646 1/2; Barren Co.; watercourse:
No Bob; Entry: John Lerty; Survey: same; Patents:
Wm Courts; white males over 21: 1; white males
16-21: 0; blacks over 16: 1; total blacks: 1; horses:
4; stud horses: 0; tavern license: 0.
Barren County Tax Book, 1800, part 1 - page: 4
FAMILY HISTORY LIBRARY film 7865
Courts, Walter,   Kentucky   Barren
County
        Courts, Walter, over 21 Male   **Color:**
        White
        slave, over 16 Male   **Color:** Colored
        slave, over 16 Male   **Color:** Colored
        slave, over 16 Male   **Color:** Colored
Acres of land: 550 1/3; Barren Co.; watercourse:
No Bob; Entry: John P. Adams; Survey: same;
Patents: same; white males over 21: 1; white males
16-21: 0; blacks over 16: 3; total blacks: 8; horses:
4; stud horses: 0; retail stores: 0; tavern license: 0.
Barren County Tax Book, 1800, part 1 - page: 4
FAMILY HISTORY LIBRARY film 7865
Courts, William,   Kentucky   Barren
County
        Courts, William,   over 21 Male
        Color: White
        slave, over 16 Male   **Color:** Colored
        slave, over 16 Male   **Color:** Colored
        slave, over 16 Male   **Color:** Colored
        slave, over 16 Male   **Color:** Colored
        slave, over 16 Male   **Color:** Colored
        slave, over 16 Male   **Color:** Colored
        slave, over 16 Male   **Color:** Colored
Acres of land: 606 2/3; Barren Co.; watercourse:
No Bob; Entry: John Lerty; Survey: same; Patents:
Wm Courts; white males over 21: 1; white males
16-21: 0; blacks over 16: 7; total blacks: 14;
horses: 8; stud horses: 0; tavern license: 0.
Barren County Tax Book, 1800, part 1 - page: 4
FAMILY HISTORY LIBRARY film 7865
Courts, Wm, Kentucky   Barren County?
        Courts, Wm,   Male
The patent for land owned by John Courts was in
his name.
Barren County Tax Book, 1800, part 1 - page: 4
FAMILY HISTORY LIBRARY film 7865
Cox, Abl, Kentucky   Barren County
        Cox, Abl,   over 21 Male   **Color:**
        White
Acres of land: 0; Barren Co.; watercourse: 0;
Entry: 0; Survey: 0; Patents: 0; white males over

21: 1; white males 16-21: 0; blacks over 16: 0; total blacks: 0; horses: 0; stud horses: 0; retail stores: 0; tavern license: 0.
Barren County Tax Book, 1800, part 1 - page: 3
FAMILY HISTORY LIBRARY film 7865
Cox, Moses, Kentucky Barren County
Cox, Moses, over 21 Male **Color:** White
Acres of land: 200; Barren Co.; watercourse: Big Barren; Entry: Moses Cox; Survey: same; Patents: 0; white males over 21: 1; white males 16-21: 0; blacks over 16: 0; total blacks: 0; horses: 1; stud horses: 0; retail stores: 0; tavern license: 0.
Barren County Tax Book, 1800, part 1 - page: 3
FAMILY HISTORY LIBRARY film 7865
Craddock, Archer, Kentucky Barren County
Craddock, Archer, over 21 Male **Color:** White
slave, over 16 Male **Color:** Colored
slave, over 16 Male **Color:** Colored
Acres of land: 595; Barren Co.; watercourse: S fork L Barren; Entry: Robt Craddock; Survey: same; Patents: same; white males over 21: 1; white males 16-21: 0; blacks over 16: 2; total blacks: 3; horses: 3; stud horses: 0; retail stores: 0; tavern: 0.
Barren County Tax Book, 1800, part 1 - page: 3
FAMILY HISTORY LIBRARY film 7865
Craddock, Robt, Kentucky Barren County?
Craddock, Robt, Male
The entry for land owned by Archer Craddock was in his name.
Barren County Tax Book, 1800, part 1 - page: 3
FAMILY HISTORY LIBRARY film 7865
Craddock, William, Kentucky Barren County
Craddock, William, 16-21 Male **Color:** White
Acres of land: 0; County: 0; watercourse: 0; Entry: 0; Survey: 0; Patent: 0; white males over 21: 0; white males 16-21: 1; blacks over 16: 0; total blacks: 0; horses: 0; stud horses: 0; tavern license: 0.
Barren County Tax Book, 1800, part 1 - page: 4
FAMILY HISTORY LIBRARY film 7865
Crawford, James, Kentucky Barren County
Crawford, James, over 21 Male **Color:** White

Acres of land: 200; Barren Co.; watercourse: Marrowbone; Entry: Thomas Minor; Survey: 0; Patents: 0; white males over 21: 1; white males 16-21: 0; blacks over 16: 0; total blacks: 0; horses: 3; stud horses: 0; tavern license: 0.
Barren County Tax Book, 1800, part 1 - page: 4
FAMILY HISTORY LIBRARY film 7865
Crawford, Jas, Kentucky Barren County?
Crawford, Jas, Male
The entry for land owned by Benjamin Mershon was in his name.
Barren County Tax Book, 1800, part 1 - page: 10
FAMILY HISTORY LIBRARY film 7865
Cray . . ., A, Kentucky Barren County?
Cray . . ., A, Male
The entry for land owned by Edmond Rogers was in the names of P. Ingraham and A Cray . . . .
Barren County Tax Book, 1800, part 1 - page: 13
FAMILY HISTORY LIBRARY film 7865
Crofford, Jas, Kentucky Barren County?
Crofford, Jas, Male
The entry for land owned by John Flint was in his name.
Barren County Tax Book, 1800, part 1 - page: 6
FAMILY HISTORY LIBRARY film 7865
Crow, John, Kentucky Barren County
Crow, John, over 21 Male **Color:** White
slave, over 16 Male **Color:** Colored
slave, over 16 Male **Color:** Colored
Acres of land: 1000; County: 0; watercourse: 0; Entry: Thomas Crow; Survey: same; Patents: same; white males over 21: 1; white males 16-21: 0; blacks over 16 2; total blacks: 4; horses: 5; stud horses: 1; retail stores: 0; tavern license: 0.
Barren County Tax Book, 1800, part 1 - page: 3
FAMILY HISTORY LIBRARY film 7865
Crow, John, Kentucky Barren County
Crow, John, Male
Acres of land: 200; Barren Co.; watercourse: little Barren; Entry: John Crow; Survey: same; Patents: 0; white males over 21: 0; white males 16-21: 0; blacks over 16: 0; total blacks: 0; horses: 0; stud horses: 0; retail stores: 0; tavern license: 0.
Barren County Tax Book, 1800, part 1 - page: 3
FAMILY HISTORY LIBRARY film 7865
Crow, John, Kentucky Barren County
Crow, John, Male

Acres of land: 200; Barren Co.; watercourse: Little Barren; Entry: Wm Robinson; Survey: same; Patents: 0; white males over 21: 0; white males 16-21: 0; blacks over 16: 0; total blacks: 0; horses: 0; stud horses: 0; retail stores: 0; tavern license: 0.
Barren County Tax Book, 1800, part 1 - page: 3
FAMILY HISTORY LIBRARY film 7865
Crow, John, Kentucky   Barren County
        Crow, John,   Male
Acres of land: 200; Barren Co.; watercourse: Little Barren; Entry: Finley; Survey: same; Patents: 0; white males over 21: 0; white males 16-21: 0; blacks over 16: 0; total blacks: 0; horses: 0; stud horses: 0; retail stores: 0; tavern license: 0.
Barren County Tax Book, 1800, part 1 - page: 3
FAMILY HISTORY LIBRARY film 7865
Crow, Thomas,   Kentucky   Barren County?
        Crow, Thomas, Male
The entry for land owned by John Crow was in his name.
Barren County Tax Book, 1800, part 1 - page: 3
FAMILY HISTORY LIBRARY film 7865
Crump, Havilich,   Kentucky   Barren County
        Crump, Havilich,   over 21 Male   **Color:** White
        slave, over 16 Male   **Color:** Colored
Acres of land: 200; Warren Co.; watercourse: Rays Branch; Entry: Havilah Crump; Survey: same; Patents: 0; white males over 21: 1; white males 16-21: 0; blacks over 16: 1; total blacks: 4; horses: 1; stud horses: 0; retail stores: 0; tavern license: 0.
Barren County Tax Book, 1800, part 1 - page: 3
FAMILY HISTORY LIBRARY film 7865
Cummins, Samuel, Kentucky   Barren County
        Cummins, Samuel,   over 21 Male   **Color:** White
Acres of land: 0; County: 0; watercourse: 0; Entry: 0; Survey: 0; Patents: 0; white males over 21: 1; white males 16-21: 0; blacks over 16: 0; total blacks: 0; horses: 3; stud horses: 0; retail stores: 0; tavern license: 0.
Barren County Tax Book, 1800, part 1 - page: 3
FAMILY HISTORY LIBRARY film 7865
Curd, Daniel, Kentucky   Barren County
        Curd, Daniel,   Male
Acres of land: 200; Barren Co.; watercourse: Beaver Creek; Entry: Sylvester Payn; Survey:

same; Patents: 0; white males over 21: 0; white males 16-21: 0; blacks over 16: 0; total blacks: 0; horses: 0; stud horses: 0; retail stores: 0; tavern license: 0.
Barren County Tax Book, 1800, part 1 - page: 3
FAMILY HISTORY LIBRARY film 7865
Curd, Daniel, Kentucky   Barren County
        Curd, Daniel,   Male
Acres of land: 200; Barren Co.; watercourse: Trace Creek; Entry: Daniel Curd; Survey: same; Patents: 0; white males over 21: 0; white males 16-21: 0; blacks over 16: 0; total blacks: 0; horses: 0; stud horses: 0; retail stores: 0; tavern license: 0.
Barren County Tax Book, 1800, part 1 - page: 3
FAMILY HISTORY LIBRARY film 7865
Curd, Daniel, Kentucky   Barren County
        Curd, Daniel,   over 21 Male   **Color:** White
        slave, over 16 Male   **Color:** Colored
Acres of land: 200; Barren Co.; watercourse: Beaver Creek; Entry: Abl Honnon; Survey: Abl Honnon; Patents: 0; white males over 21: 1; white males 16-21: 0; blacks over 16: 1; total blacks: 3; horses: 4; stud horses: 0; retail stores: 0; tavern license: 0.
Barren County Tax Book, 1800, part 1 - page: 3
FAMILY HISTORY LIBRARY film 7865
Dale, Isaac, Kentucky   Barren County
        Dale, Isaac,   over 21 Male   **Color:** White
        Dale,   16-21   Male   **Color:** White
Acres of land: 200; Barren Co.; watercourse: Bens Creek; Entry: Isaac Dale; Survey: same; Patent: 0; white males over 21: 1; white males 16-21: 1; blacks over 16: 0; total blacks: 1; horses: 3; stud horses: 0; tavern license: 0.
Barren County Tax Book, 1800, part 1 - page: 4
FAMILY HISTORY LIBRARY film 7865
Dale, Reubin, Kentucky   Barren County
        Dale, Reubin,   over 21 Male   **Color:** White
Acres of land: 200; Barren Co.; watercourse: Whiteoak Creek; Entry: Reubin Dale; Survey: same; Patent: 0; white males over 21: 1; white males 16-21: 0; blacks over 16: 0; total blacks: 0; horses: 1; stud horses: 0; tavern license: 0.
Barren County Tax Book, 1800, part 1 - page: 4
FAMILY HISTORY LIBRARY film 7865
Davis, Jonathan,   Kentucky   Barren County

Davis, Jonathan, over 21 Male
Color: White
Acres of land: 0; County: 0; watercourse: 0; Entry: 0; Survey: 0; Patent: 0; white males over 21: 1; white males 16-21: 0; blacks over 16: 0; total blacks: 0; horses: 1; stud horses: 0; retail stores: 0; tavern license: 0.
Barren County Tax Book, 1800, part 1 - page: 5
FAMILY HISTORY LIBRARY film 7865
Davis, Saml, Kentucky Barren County?
Davis, Saml, Male
The entry for land owned by Samuel Renick senr was in his name.
Barren County Tax Book, 1800, part 1 - page: 13
FAMILY HISTORY LIBRARY film 7865
Defevers, John, Kentucky Barren County
Defevers, John, over 21 Male **Color:** White
Acres of land: 200; Barren Co.; watercourse: Green River; Entry: Sarah Cotney; Survey: same; Patent: 0; white males over 21: 1; white males 16-21: 0; blacks over 16: 0; total blacks: 0; horses: 5; stud horses: 0; retail stores: 0; tavern license: 0.
Barren County Tax Book, 1800, part 1 - page: 5
FAMILY HISTORY LIBRARY film 7865
Dement, Charles, Kentucky Barren County
Dement, Charles, over 21 Male
Color: White
Acres of land: 0; County: 0; watercourse: 0; Entry: 0; Survey: 0; Patent: 0; white males over 21: 1; white males 16-21: 0; blacks over 16: 0; total blacks: 0; horses: 1; stud horses: 0; retail stores: 0; tavern license: 0.
Barren County Tax Book, 1800, part 1 - page: 5
FAMILY HISTORY LIBRARY film 7865
Dennis, Joseph, Kentucky Barren County
Dennis, Joseph, over 21 Male
Color: White
Acres of land: 100; Barren Co.; watercourse: No Bob; Entry: Joseph Dennis; Survey: same; Patent: 0; white males over 21: 1; white males 16-21: 0; blacks over 16: 0; total blacks: 0; horses: 3; stud horses: 0; retail stores: 0; tavern license: 0.
Barren County Tax Book, 1800, part 1 - page: 5
FAMILY HISTORY LIBRARY film 7865
Dick, Abraham, Kentucky Barren County

Dick, Abraham, over 21 Male
Color: White
Acres of land: 200; Barren Co.; watercourse: Little Barren; Entry: Abraham Dick; Survey: same; Patent: 0; white males over 21: 1; white males 16-21: 0; blacks over 16: 0; total blacks: 0; horses: 1; stud horses: 0; retail stores: 0; tavern license: 0.
Barren County Tax Book, 1800, part 1 - page: 5
FAMILY HISTORY LIBRARY film 7865
Dickerson, Solamon, Kentucky Barren County
Dickerson, Solamon, over 21 Male
Color: White
Dickerson, 16-21 Male **Color:** White
Acres of land: 0; County: 0; watercourse: 0; Entry: 0; Survey: 0; Patent: 0; white males over 21: 1; white males 16-21: 1; blacks over 16: 0; total blacks: 0; horses: 1?; stud horses: 0; retail stores: 0; tavern license: 0.
Barren County Tax Book, 1800, part 1 - page: 5
FAMILY HISTORY LIBRARY film 7865
Dixon, David, Kentucky Barren County
Dixon, David, over 21 Male **Color:** White
Acres of land: 100; Barren Co.; watercourse: Sulphur lick Creek; Entry: David Dixon; Survey: same; Patent: 0; white males over 21: 1; white males 16-21: 0; blacks over 16: 0; total blacks: 0; horses: 4; stud horses: 0; retail stores: 0; tavern license: 0.
Barren County Tax Book, 1800, part 1 - page: 5
FAMILY HISTORY LIBRARY film 7865
Doke, James, Kentucky Barren County?
Doke, James, Male
The entry for land owned by John A Holady was in his name.
Barren County Tax Book, 1800, part 1 - page: 7
FAMILY HISTORY LIBRARY film 7865
Dooly, Abner, Kentucky Barren County
Dooly, Abner, over 21 Male **Color:** White
Acres of land: 200; Barren Co.; watercourse: Little Barren; Entry: Abner Dooly; Survey: same; Patent: 0; white males over 21: 1; white males 16-21: 0; blacks over 16: 0; total blacks: 0; horses: 3; stud horses: 0; retail stores: 0; tavern license: 0.
Barren County Tax Book, 1800, part 1 - page: 5
FAMILY HISTORY LIBRARY film 7865

Dooly, George, Kentucky Barren County
Dooly, George, over 21 Male **Color:** White
Acres of land: 200; Barren Co.; watercourse: Little Barren; Entry: Geo Dooly; Survey: same; Patent: 0; white males over 21: 1; white males 16-21: 0; blacks over 16: 0; total blacks: 0; horses: 2; stud horses: 0; retail stores: 0; tavern license: 0.
Barren County Tax Book, 1800, part 1 - page: 5
FAMILY HISTORY LIBRARY film 7865

Dooly, Moses, Junr Kentucky Barren County
Dooly, Moses, Junr over 21 Male **Color:** White
Acres of land: 200; Barren Co.; watercourse: Marrowbone; Entry: Moses Dooly; Survey: same; Patent: 0; white males over 21: 1; white males 16-21: 0; blacks over 16: 0; total blacks: 0; horses: 2; stud horses: 0; retail stores: 0; tavern license: 0.
Barren County Tax Book, 1800, part 1 - page: 5
FAMILY HISTORY LIBRARY film 7865

Dooly, Moses, Senr Kentucky Barren County
Dooly, Moses, Senr Male
Acres of land: 200; Barren Co.; watercourse: 0; Entry: Thomas Dooly; Survey: same; Patent: 0; white males over 21: 0; white males 16-21: 0; blacks over 16: 0; total blacks: 0; horses: 0; stud horses: 0; retail stores: 0; tavern license: 0.
Barren County Tax Book, 1800, part 1 - page: 5
FAMILY HISTORY LIBRARY film 7865

Dooly, Moses, Senr Kentucky Barren County
Dooly, Moses, Senr over 21 Male **Color:** White
Dooly, 16-21 Male **Color:** White
Acres of land: 200; Barren Co.; watercourse: Little Barren; Entry: Moses Dooly; Survey: same; Patent: 0; white males over 21: 1; white males 16-21: 1; blacks over 16: 0; total blacks: 0; horses: 6; stud horses: 1; retail stores: 0; tavern license: 0.
Barren County Tax Book, 1800, part 1 - page: 5
FAMILY HISTORY LIBRARY film 7865

Dooly, Reubin, Kentucky Barren County
Dooly, Reubin, over 21 Male **Color:** White
Acres of land: 200; Barren Co.; watercourse: Little Barren; Entry: Reubin Dooly; Survey: same;

Patent: 0; white males over 21: 1; white males 16-21: 0; blacks over 16: 0; total blacks: 0; horses: 3; stud horses: 0; retail stores: 0; tavern license: 0.
Barren County Tax Book, 1800, part 1 - page: 5
FAMILY HISTORY LIBRARY film 7865

Dooly, Thomas, Kentucky Barren County?
Dooly, Thomas, Male
The entry for land owned by Moses Dooly Senr was in his name.
Barren County Tax Book, 1800, part 1 - page: 5
FAMILY HISTORY LIBRARY film 7865

Dougherty, Robert, Kentucky Barren County
Dougherty, Robert, over 21 Male **Color:** White
slave, over 16 Male **Color:** Colored
Acres of land: 100; Barren Co.; watercourse: Fallen Timber; Entry: Robert Dougherty; Survey: same; Patent: 0; white males over 21: 1; white males 16-21: 0; blacks over 16: 1; total blacks: 3; horses: 6; stud horses: 1; tavern license: 0.
Barren County Tax Book, 1800, part 1 - page: 4
FAMILY HISTORY LIBRARY film 7865

Douglass, John, Kentucky Barren County
Douglass, John, over 21 Male **Color:** White
Acres of land: 200; Barren Co.; watercourse: Marrowbone; Entry: John Douglass; Survey: same; Patent: 0; white males over 21: 1; white males 16-21: 0; blacks over 16: 0; total blacks: 0; horses: 1; stud horses: 0; retail stores: 0; tavern license: 0.
Barren County Tax Book, 1800, part 1 - page: 5
FAMILY HISTORY LIBRARY film 7865

Douglass, William, Kentucky Barren County
Douglass, William, over 21 Male **Color:** White
Acres of land: 200; Barren Co.; watercourse: Cumberland; Entry: Wm Douglass; Survey: same; Patent: same; white males over 21: 1; white males 16-21: 0; blacks over 16: 0; total blacks: 0; horses: 1; stud horses: 0; retail stores: 0; tavern license: 0.
Barren County Tax Book, 1800, part 1 - page: 5
FAMILY HISTORY LIBRARY film 7865

Downy, Ezekiel, Kentucky Barren County
Downy, Ezekiel, over 21 Male **Color:** White

Acres of land: 200; Barren Co.; watercourse: Clay Creek; Entry: William Matthews; Survey: Ezekiel Downy; Patent: 0; white males over 21: 1; white males 16-21: 0; blacks over 16: 0; total blacks: 0; horses: 3; stud horses: 0; retail stores: 0; tavern: 0.
Barren County Tax Book, 1800, part 1 - page: 5
FAMILY HISTORY LIBRARY film 7865

Doyal, James, Kentucky   Barren County
Doyal, James,   over 21 Male   **Color:** White
Acres of land: 100; Barren Co.; watercourse: Coles fork; Entry: James Doyal; Survey: same; Patent: 0; white males over 21: 1; white males 16-21: 0; blacks over 16: 0; total blacks: 0; horses: 3; stud horses: 0; retail stores: 0; tavern license: 0.
Barren County Tax Book, 1800, part 1 - page: 5
FAMILY HISTORY LIBRARY film 7865

Druse?, Edm, Kentucky   Barren County?
Druse?, Edm,   Male
The entry for land owned by Edmond Rogers was in the names of E Rogers and Edm Druse?.
Barren County Tax Book, 1800, part 1 - page: 13
FAMILY HISTORY LIBRARY film 7865

Ducart?, Elisha,   Kentucky   Barren County
Ducart?, Elisha,   over 21 Male   **Color:** White
Ducart?,   16-21   Male   **Color:** White
Acres of land: 200; Barren Co.; watercourse: Bluespring? Creek?; Entry: Elisha Ducart?; Survey: same; Patent: 0; white males over 21: 1; white males 16-21: 1; blacks over 16: 0; total blacks: 0; horses: 4; stud horses: 0; tavern license: 0.
Barren County Tax Book, 1800, part 1 - page: 4
FAMILY HISTORY LIBRARY film 7865

Duncan, William,   Kentucky   Barren County
Duncan, William,   over 21 Male   **Color:** White
Acres of land: 0; County: 0; watercourse: 0; Entry: 0; Survey: 0; Patent: 0; white males over 21: 1; white males 16-21: 0; blacks over 16: 0; total blacks: 0; horses: 2; stud horses: 0; tavern license: 0.
Barren County Tax Book, 1800, part 1 - page: 4
FAMILY HISTORY LIBRARY film 7865

Eastridge, Abrm,   Kentucky   Barren County?
Eastridge, Abrm,   Male
The patent for land owned by William Handy was in his name.
Barren County Tax Book, 1800, part 1 - page: 8
FAMILY HISTORY LIBRARY film 7865

Eaton, James, Kentucky   Barren County
Eaton, James,   over 21 Male   **Color:** White
Acres of land: 200; Barren Co.; watercourse: 0; Entry: 0; Survey: 0; Patent: 0; white males over 21: 1; white males 16-21: 0; blacks over 16: 0; total blacks: 0; horses: 1; stud horses: 0; retail stores: 0; tavern license: 0.
Barren County Tax Book, 1800, part 1 - page: 5
FAMILY HISTORY LIBRARY film 7865

Edgar, John, Kentucky   Barren County
Edgar, John,   over 21 Male   **Color:** White
Acres of land: 0; County: 0; watercourse: 0; Entry: 0; Survey: 0; Patent: 0; white males over 21: 1; white males 16-21: 0; blacks over 16: 0; total blacks: 0; horses: 2; stud horses: 0; retail stores: 0; tavern license: 0.
Barren County Tax Book, 1800, part 1 - page: 5
FAMILY HISTORY LIBRARY film 7865

Edwards, Alexander, Kentucky   Barren County
Edwards, Alexander,   over 21 Male   **Color:** White
Acres of land: 200; Barren Co.; watercourse: Bone Creek; Entry: Alexander Edwards; Survey: same; Patent: 0; white males over 21: 1; white males 16-21: 0; blacks over 16: 0; total blacks: 0; horses: 3; stud horses: 0; retail stores: 0; tavern license: 0.
Barren County Tax Book, 1800, part 1 - page: 5
FAMILY HISTORY LIBRARY film 7865

Edwards, Cadar,   Kentucky   Barren County
Edwards, Cadar,   over 21 Male   **Color:** White
Acres of land: 0; County: 0; watercourse: 0; Entry: 0; Survey: 0; Patent: 0; white males over 21: 1; white males 16-21: 0; blacks over 16: 0; total blacks: 0; horses: 1; stud horses: 0; retail stores: 0; tavern license: 0.
Barren County Tax Book, 1800, part 1 - page: 5
FAMILY HISTORY LIBRARY film 7865

Edwards, William,   Kentucky   Barren County?

Edwards, William,   over 21 Male
Color: White
Edwards,   over 21 Male   **Color:**
White
Acres of land: 0; County: 0; watercourse: 0; Entry: 0; Survey: 0; Patent: 0; white males over 21: 2; white males 16-21: 0; blacks over 16: 0; total blacks: 0; horses: 1; stud horses: 0; retail stores: 0; tavern license: 0.
Barren County Tax Book, 1800, part 1 - page: 5
FAMILY HISTORY LIBRARY film 7865
Elliott, John,   Kentucky   Barren County
Elliott, John,   over 21 Male   **Color:**
White
Acres of land: 0; County: 0; watercourse: 0; Entry: 0; Survey: 0; Patent: 0; white males over 21: 1; white males 16-21: 0; blacks over 16: 0; total blacks: 0; horses: 0; stud horses: 0; retail stores: 0; tavern license: 0.
Barren County Tax Book, 1800, part 1 - page: 5
FAMILY HISTORY LIBRARY film 7865
Evans, Thomas,   Kentucky   Barren
County
Evans, Thomas,   over 21 Male
Color: White
Acres of land: 0; County: 0; watercourse: 0; Entry: 0; Survey: 0; Patent: 0; white males over 21: 1; white males 16-21: 0; blacks over 16: 0; total blacks: 0; horses: 2; stud horses: 0; retail stores: 0; tavern license: 0.
Barren County Tax Book, 1800, part 1 - page: 5
FAMILY HISTORY LIBRARY film 7865
Feland, Thos, Kentucky   Barren County?
Feland, Thos,   Male
The entry for land owned by William Feland was in his name.
Barren County Tax Book, 1800, part 1 - page: 5
FAMILY HISTORY LIBRARY film 7865
Feland, William,   Kentucky   Barren
County
Feland, William,   Male
Acres of land: 200; Barren Co.; watercourse: Fallen Timber; Entry: 0; Survey: 0; Patent: 0; white males over 21: 0; white males 16-21: 0; blacks over 16: 0; total blacks: 0; horses: 0; stud horses: 0; retail stores: 0; tavern license: 0.
Barren County Tax Book, 1800, part 1 - page: 5
FAMILY HISTORY LIBRARY film 7865
Feland, William,   Kentucky   Barren
County

Feland, William,   Male
Acres of land: 28; Barren Co.; watercourse: Fallen Timber; Entry: John Smith; Survey: Wm Feland & D. Warren; Patent: 0; white males over 21: 0; white males 16-21: 0; blacks over 16: 0; total blacks: 0; horses: 0; stud horses: 0; tavern: 0.
Barren County Tax Book, 1800, part 1 - page: 5
FAMILY HISTORY LIBRARY film 7865
Feland, William,   Kentucky   Barren
County
Feland, William,   over 21 Male
Color: White
slave, over 16 Male   **Color:** Colored
Acres of land: 2000; Gallatin Co.; watercourse: Locust Creek; Entry: Thos Feland; Survey: Wm Feland; Patent: 0; white males over 21: 1; white males 16-21: 0; blacks over 16: 1; total blacks: 2; horses: 3; stud horses: 0; retail store: 0; tavern: 0.
Barren County Tax Book, 1800, part 1 - page: 5
FAMILY HISTORY LIBRARY film 7865
Fields, Robert,   Kentucky   Barren
County
Fields, Robert, over 21 Male   **Color:**
White
Fields, 16-21 Male   **Color:** White
Acres of land: 200; Barren Co.; watercourse: 0; Entry: 0; Survey: 0; Patent: 0; white males over 21: 1; white males 16-21: 1; blacks over 16: 0; total blacks: 2; horses: 5; stud horses: 0; retail stores: 0; tavern license: 0.
Barren County Tax Book, 1800, part 1 - page: 6
FAMILY HISTORY LIBRARY film 7865
Finley, Kentucky   Barren County?
Finley, Male
The entry for land owned by John Crow was in his name.
Barren County Tax Book, 1800, part 1 - page: 3
FAMILY HISTORY LIBRARY film 7865
Fleming, John,   Kentucky   Barren
County
Fleming, John, over 21 Male   **Color:**
White
Acres of land: 0; County: 0; watercourse: 0; Entry: 0; Survey: 0; Patent: 0; white males over 21: 1; white males 16-21: 0; blacks over 16: 0; total blacks: 0; horses: 1; stud horses: 0; retail stores: 0; tavern license: 0.
Barren County Tax Book, 1800, part 1 - page: 5
FAMILY HISTORY LIBRARY film 7865

Fletcher, Geo W, Kentucky Barren County

Fletcher, Geo W, Male

Acres of land: 0; County: 0; watercourse: 0; Entry: 0; Survey: 0; Patent: 0; white males over 21: 1; white males 16-21: 0; blacks over 16: 0; total blacks: 1; horses: 3; stud horses: 0; retail stores: 0; tavern license: 0.

Barren County Tax Book, 1800, part 1 - page: 6
FAMILY HISTORY LIBRARY film 7865

Flint, John, Kentucky Barren County

Flint, John, over 21 Male **Color:** White

Acres of land: 125 1/4; Barren Co.; watercourse: Green River; Entry: Jas Crofford; Survey: same; Patent: 0; white males over 21: 1; white males 16-21: 0; blacks over 16: 0; total blacks: 0; horses: 3; stud horses: 0; retail stores: 0; tavern license: 1.

Barren County Tax Book, 1800, part 1 - page: 6
FAMILY HISTORY LIBRARY film 7865

Flint, John, Kentucky Barren County

Flint, John, Male

Acres of land: 100; Barren Co.; watercourse: Little Barren; Entry: Michael Campbell; Survey: same; Patent: 0; white males over 21: 0; white males 16-21: 0; blacks over 16: 0; total blacks: 0; horses: 0; stud horses: 0; retail stores: 0; tavern license: 0.

Barren County Tax Book, 1800, part 1 - page: 6
FAMILY HISTORY LIBRARY film 7865

Fliping, Thomas, Kentucky Barren County

Fliping, Thomas, Male

Acres of land: 200; Barren Co.; watercourse: Indian Creek; Entry: Thos Fliping; Survey: same; Patent: 0; white males over 21: 0; white males 16-21: 0; blacks over 16: 0; total blacks: 0; horses: 0; stud horses: 0; retail stores: 0; tavern license: 0.

Barren County Tax Book, 1800, part 1 - page: 6
FAMILY HISTORY LIBRARY film 7865

Fliping, Thomas, Kentucky Barren County

Fliping, Thomas, Male

Acres of land: 200; Barren Co.; watercourse: Bagen Creek?; Entry: Thos Fliping; Survey: same; Patent: 0; white males over 21: 0; white males 16-21: 0; blacks over 16: 0; total blacks: 0; horses: 0; stud horses: 0; retail stores: 0; tavern license: 0.

Barren County Tax Book, 1800, part 1 - page: 6
FAMILY HISTORY LIBRARY film 7865

Fliping, Thomas, Kentucky Barren County

Fliping, Thomas, over 21 Male **Color:** White

Fliping, 16-21 Male **Color:** White

Fliping, 16-21 Male **Color:** White

slave, over 16 Male **Color:** Colored

slave, over 16 Male **Color:** Colored

slave, over 16 Male **Color:** Colored

Acres of land: 200; Barren Co.; watercourse: Indian Creek; Entry: Thos Fliping; Survey: same; Patent: 0; white males over 21: 1; white males 16-21: 2; blacks over 16: 3; total blacks: 7; horses: 5; stud horses: 0; retail stores: 0; tavern license: 0.

Barren County Tax Book, 1800, part 1 - page: 6
FAMILY HISTORY LIBRARY film 7865

Fliping, Thomas, Kentucky Barren County

Fliping, Thomas, Male

Acres of land: 200; Barren Co.; watercourse: Indian Creek; Entry: Thos Fliping; Survey: same; Patent: 0; white males over 21: 0; white males 16-21: 0; blacks over 16: 0; total blacks: 0; horses: 0; stud horses: 0; retail stores: 0; tavern license: 0.

Barren County Tax Book, 1800, part 1 - page: 6
FAMILY HISTORY LIBRARY film 7865

Fliping, Thomas, Kentucky Barren County

Fliping, Thomas, Male

Acres of land: 200; Barren Co.; watercourse: Indian Creek; Entry: Thos Neal; Survey: Thos Fliping; Patent: 0; white males over 21: 0; white males 16-21: 0; blacks over 16: 0; total blacks: 0; horses: 0; stud horses: 0; retail stores: 0; tavern license: 0.

Barren County Tax Book, 1800, part 1 - page: 6
FAMILY HISTORY LIBRARY film 7865

Fliping, Thomas, Kentucky Barren County

Fliping, Thomas, Male

Acres of land: 200; Barren Co.; watercourse: Indian Creek; Entry: Thos Fliping; Survey: same; Patent: 0; white males over 21: 0; white males 16-21: 0; blacks over 16: 0; total blacks: 0; horses: 0; stud horses: 0; retail stores: 0; tavern license: 0.

Barren County Tax Book, 1800, part 1 - page: 6
FAMILY HISTORY LIBRARY film 7865

Fliping, Thomas, Kentucky Barren County

Fliping, Thomas, Male

Acres of land: 200; Barren Co.; watercourse: Indian Creek; Entry: Thos Fliping; Survey: same; Patent: 0; white males over 21: 0; white males 16-21: 0; blacks over 16: 0; total blacks: 0; horses: 0; stud horses: 0; retail stores: 0; tavern license: 0.

Barren County Tax Book, 1800, part 1 - page: 6
FAMILY HISTORY LIBRARY film 7865

Forbes, James, Kentucky Barren County?

Forbes, James, Male

The entry for land owned by Henry Cook was in his name.

Barren County Tax Book, 1800, part 1 - page: 3
FAMILY HISTORY LIBRARY film 7865

Forbes, Robt, Kentucky Barren County?

Forbes, Robt, Male

The entry for land owned by Henry Cook was in his name.

Barren County Tax Book, 1800, part 1 - page: 3
FAMILY HISTORY LIBRARY film 7865

Forbis, James, Kentucky Barren County

Forbis, James, over 21 Male **Color:** White

Acres of land: 0; County: 0; watercourse: 0; Entry: 0; Survey: 0; Patent: 0; white males over 21: 1; white males 16-21: 0; blacks over 16: 0; total blacks: 1; horses: 2; stud horses: 0; retail stores: 0; tavern license: 0.

Barren County Tax Book, 1800, part 1 - page: 5
FAMILY HISTORY LIBRARY film 7865

Forbis, James, Jnr Kentucky Barren County

Forbis, James, Jnr over 21 Male **Color:** White

Acres of land: 0; County: 0; watercourse: 0; Entry: 0; Survey: 0; Patent: 0; white males over 21: 1; white males 16-21: 0; blacks over 16: 0; total blacks: 0; horses: 2; stud horses: 0; retail stores: 0; tavern license: 0.

Barren County Tax Book, 1800, part 1 - page: 6
FAMILY HISTORY LIBRARY film 7865

Forbis, John, Kentucky Barren County

Forbis, John, Male

Acres of land: 200; Barren Co.; watercourse: Little Barren; Entry: John Forbis; Survey: same; Patent: 0; white males over 21: 1; white males 16-21: 0; blacks over 16: 0; total blacks: 0; horses: 3; stud horses: 0; retail stores: 0; tavern license: 0.

Barren County Tax Book, 1800, part 1 - page: 6
FAMILY HISTORY LIBRARY film 7865

Forbis, John, Kentucky Barren County

Forbis, John, over 21 Male **Color:** White

Forbis, over 21 Male **Color:** White

Forbis, 16-21 Male **Color:** White

Acres of land: 200; Barren Co.; watercourse: Little Barren; Entry: John Forbis; Survey: same; Patent: 0; white males over 21: 2; white males 16-21: 1; blacks over 16: 0; total blacks: 0; horses: 7; stud horses: 0; retail stores: 0; tavern license: 0.

Barren County Tax Book, 1800, part 1 - page: 6
FAMILY HISTORY LIBRARY film 7865

Fortner, Thomas, Kentucky Barren County

Fortner, Thomas, over 21 Male **Color:** White

Acres of land: 0; County: 0; watercourse: 0; Entry: 0; Survey: 0; Patent: 0; white males over 21: 1; white males 16-21: 0; blacks over 16: 0; total blacks: 0; horses: 1; stud horses: 0; retail stores: 0; tavern license: 0.

Barren County Tax Book, 1800, part 1 - page: 6
FAMILY HISTORY LIBRARY film 7865

Fortner, Thos, Kentucky Barren County?

Fortner, Thos, Male

The entry for land owned by Ferdinand Hamilton was in his name.

Barren County Tax Book, 1800, part 1 - page: 8
FAMILY HISTORY LIBRARY film 7865

Franklin, John, Kentucky Barren County

Franklin, John, over 21 Male **Color:** White

Acres of land: 0; County: 0; watercourse: 0; Entry: 0; Survey: 0; Patent: 0; white males over 21: 1; white males 16-21: 0; blacks over 16: 0; total blacks: 0; horses: 1; stud horses: 0; retail stores: 0; tavern license: 0.

Barren County Tax Book, 1800, part 1 - page: 5
FAMILY HISTORY LIBRARY film 7865

Frayser?, Martin, Kentucky Barren County?

Frayser?, Martin, Male

The entry for land owned by John Berks Senr was in his name.

Barren County Tax Book, 1800, part 1 - page: 1
FAMILY HISTORY LIBRARY film 7865
French, Benjamin, Kentucky Barren County
    French, Benjamin, over 21 Male
    Color: White
Acres of land: 0; County: 0; watercourse: 0; Entry: 0; Survey: 0; Patent: 0; white males over 21: 1; white males 16-21: 0; blacks over 16: 0; total blacks: 0; horses: 0; stud horses: 0; retail stores: 0; tavern license: 0.
Barren County Tax Book, 1800, part 1 - page: 5
FAMILY HISTORY LIBRARY film 7865
Garnett, John, Kentucky Barren County
    Garnett, John, Male
Acres of land: 200; Barren Co.; watercourse: W Bluespring Creek; Entry: John Garnett; Survey: 0; Patent: 0; white males over 21: 0; white males 16-21: 0; blacks over 16: 0; total blacks: 0; horses: 0; stud horses: 0; retail stores: 0; tavern license: 0.
Barren County Tax Book, 1800, part 1 - page: 6
FAMILY HISTORY LIBRARY film 7865
Garnett, John, Kentucky Barren County
    Garnett, John, Male
Acres of land: 200; Barren Co.; watercourse: Bluespring Creek; Entry: John Garnett; Survey: same; Patent: same; white males over 21: 0; white males 16-21: 0; blacks over 16: 0; total blacks: 0; horses: 0; stud horses: 0; retail store: 0; tavern: 0.
Barren County Tax Book, 1800, part 1 - page: 6
FAMILY HISTORY LIBRARY film 7865
Garnett, John, Kentucky Barren County
    Garnett, John, Male
Acres of land: 250; Washington Co.; watercourse: Beech fork; Entry: John Garnett; Survey: same; Patent: 0; white males over 21: 0; white males 16-21: 0; blacks over 16: 0; total blacks: 0; horses: 0; stud horses: 0; retail stores: 0; tavern license: 0.
Barren County Tax Book, 1800, part 1 - page: 6
FAMILY HISTORY LIBRARY film 7865
Garnett, John, Kentucky Barren County?
    Garnett, John, Male
The entry for land owned by Edward Gill was in his name.
Barren County Tax Book, 1800, part 1 - page: 6
FAMILY HISTORY LIBRARY film 7865
Garnett, John, Kentucky Barren County
    Garnett, John, over 21 Male **Color:** White

Garnett, over 21 Male **Color:** White
Garnett, over 21 Male **Color:** White
slave, over 16 Male **Color:** Colored
slave, over 16 Male **Color:** Colored
slave, over 16 Male **Color:** Colored
slave, over 16 Male **Color:** Colored
slave, over 16 Male **Color:** Colored
Acres of land: 2000; Barren Co.; watercourse: Fallen Timber; Entry: Edmond Rogers; Survey: same; Patent: same; white males over 21: 3; white males 16-21: 0; blacks over 16: 5; total blacks: 6; horses: 12; stud horses: 1; retail store: 0; tavern: 0.
Barren County Tax Book, 1800, part 1 - page: 6
FAMILY HISTORY LIBRARY film 7865
Garnett, John, Kentucky Barren County
    Garnett, John, Male
Acres of land: 200; Barren Co.; watercourse: Bluespring Creek; Entry: Wm Renick?; Survey: John Garnett; Patent: same; white males over 21: 0; white males 16-21: 0; blacks over 16: 0; total blacks: 0; horses: 0; stud horses: 0; retail store: 0; tavern: 0.
Barren County Tax Book, 1800, part 1 - page: 6
FAMILY HISTORY LIBRARY film 7865
Gee, Jesse, Kentucky Barren County
    Gee, Jesse, over 21 Male **Color:** White
    slave, over 16 Male **Color:** Colored
    slave, over 16 Male **Color:** Colored
    slave, over 16 Male **Color:** Colored
Acres of land: 150; Barren Co.; watercourse: Glovers Creek; Entry: Jesse Gee; Survey: same; Patent: 0; white males over 21: 1; white males 16-21: 0; blacks over 16: 3; total blacks: 5; horses: 6; stud horses: 0; retail stores: 0; tavern license: 0.
Barren County Tax Book, 1800, part 1 - page: 7
FAMILY HISTORY LIBRARY film 7865
Gest, Joseph, Kentucky Barren County
    Gest, Joseph, over 21 Male **Color:** White
    Gest, 16-21 Male **Color:** White
Acres of land: 200; Barren Co.; watercourse: Line Creek; Entry: Joseph Gest; Survey: same; Patent: 0; white males over 21: 1; white males 16-21: 1; blacks over 16: 0; total blacks: 0; horses: 5; stud horses: 0; retail stores: 0; tavern license: 0.
Barren County Tax Book, 1800, part 1 - page: 7
FAMILY HISTORY LIBRARY film 7865

Gest, Thomas, Kentucky   Barren County
        Gest, Thomas, over 21 Male   **Color:**
        White
Acres of land: 108; Barren Co.; watercourse: Line
Creek; Entry: Thos Gest; Survey: same; Patent: 0;
white males over 21: 1; white males 16-21: 0;
blacks over 16: 0; total blacks: 0; horses: 1; stud
horses: 0; retail stores: 0; tavern license: 0.
Barren County Tax Book, 1800, part 1 - page: 7
FAMILY HISTORY LIBRARY film 7865

Gest, William, Kentucky   Barren County
        Gest, William, over 21 Male   **Color:**
        White
Acres of land: 200; Christian Co.; watercourse:
Sinking fork Little Barren?; Entry: William Gest;
Survey: same; Patent: 0; white males over 21: 1;
white males 16-21: 0; blacks over 16: 0; total
blacks: 0; horses: 0; stud horses: 1; tavern: 0.
Barren County Tax Book, 1800, part 1 - page: 7
FAMILY HISTORY LIBRARY film 7865

Gest, William, Kentucky   Barren County
        Gest, William, Male
Acres of land: 100; Christian Co.; watercourse:
Sinking fork Little Barren?; Entry: William Gest;
Survey: same; Patent: 0; white males over 21: 0;
white males 16-21: 0; blacks over 16: 0; total
blacks: 0; horses: 0; stud horses: 0; tavern: 0.
Barren County Tax Book, 1800, part 1 - page: 7
FAMILY HISTORY LIBRARY film 7865

Gest, William, Kentucky   Barren County
        Gest, William, over 21 Male   **Color:**
        White
        slave, over 16 Male   **Color:** Colored
Acres of land: 0; County: 0; watercourse: 0; Entry:
0; Survey: 0; Patent: 0; white males over 21: 1;
white males 16-21: 0; blacks over 16: 1; total
blacks: 1; horses: 1; stud horses: 0; retail stores: 0;
tavern license: 0.
Barren County Tax Book, 1800, part 1 - page: 7
FAMILY HISTORY LIBRARY film 7865

Gill, Edward, Kentucky   Barren County
        Gill, Edward, over 21 Male   **Color:**
        White
Acres of land: 200; Barren Co.; watercourse: Wh
O Creek; Entry: John Garnett; Survey: 0; Patent: 0;
white males over 21: 1; white males 16-21: 0;
blacks over 16: 0; total blacks: 0; horses: 2; stud
horses: 0; retail stores: 0; tavern license: 0.
Barren County Tax Book, 1800, part 1 - page: 6
FAMILY HISTORY LIBRARY film 7865

Gill, Wm, Jnr Kentucky   Barren County?
        Gill, Wm, Jnr   Male
The entry for land owned by John Robinson was in
his name.
Barren County Tax Book, 1800, part 1 - page: 13
FAMILY HISTORY LIBRARY film 7865

Gill, Wm, Senr Kentucky   Barren County?
        Gill, Wm, Senr Male
The entry for land owned by John Robinson was in
his name.
Barren County Tax Book, 1800, part 1 - page: 13
FAMILY HISTORY LIBRARY film 7865

Gilleland, John,   Kentucky   Barren
County
        Gilleland, John,   over 21 Male
        Color: White
Acres of land: 0; County: 0; watercourse: 0; Entry:
0; Survey: 0; Patent: 0; white males over 21: 1;
white males 16-21: 0; blacks over 16: 0; total
blacks: 0; horses: 4; stud horses: 0; retail stores: 0;
tavern license: 0.
Barren County Tax Book, 1800, part 1 - page: 7
FAMILY HISTORY LIBRARY film 7865

Gilleland, Jonathan, Kentucky   Barren
County
        Gilleland, Jonathan,   over 21 Male
        Color: White
Acres of land: 0; County: 0; watercourse: 0; Entry:
0; Survey: 0; Patent: 0; white males over 21: 1;
white males 16-21: 0; blacks over 16: 0; total
blacks: 0; horses: 2; stud horses: 0; retail stores: 0;
tavern license: 0.
Barren County Tax Book, 1800, part 1 - page: 7
FAMILY HISTORY LIBRARY film 7865

Gillock, Larrance,   Kentucky   Barren
County
        Gillock, Larrance,   over 21 Male
        Color: White
Acres of land: 0; County: 0; watercourse: 0; Entry:
0; Survey: 0; Patent: 0; white males over 21: 1;
white males 16-21: 0; blacks over 16: 0; total
blacks: 0; horses: 4; stud horses: 0; retail stores: 0;
tavern license: 0.
Barren County Tax Book, 1800, part 1 - page: 7
FAMILY HISTORY LIBRARY film 7865

Gipson, Jacob,   Kentucky   Barren
County
        Gipson, Jacob, over 21 Male   **Color:**
        White

Acres of land: 100; Barren Co.; watercourse: Fallen Timber; Entry: John Tony; Survey: same; Patent: 0; white males over 21: 1; white males 16-21: 0; blacks over 16: 0; total blacks: 0; horses: 5; stud horses: 0; retail stores: 0; tavern license: 0.
Barren County Tax Book, 1800, part 1 - page: 6
FAMILY HISTORY LIBRARY film 7865

Goff, John,   Kentucky   Barren County
    Goff, John,   over 21 Male   **Color:** White
    Goff,   16-21   Male   **Color:** White
    Goff,   16-21   Male   **Color:** White
Acres of land: 100; Barren Co.; watercourse: Little Barren; Entry: John Goff; Survey: same; Patent: 0; white males over 21: 1; white males 16-21: 2; blacks over 16: 0; total blacks: 0; horses: 2; stud horses: 0; retail stores: 0; tavern license: 0.
Barren County Tax Book, 1800, part 1 - page: 6
FAMILY HISTORY LIBRARY film 7865

Goforth, Andrew,   Kentucky   Barren County
    Goforth, Andrew,   over 21 Male   **Color:** White
Acres of land: 200; Barren Co.; watercourse: Coles Creek; Entry: Andrew Goforth; Survey: same; Patent: 0; white males over 21: 1; white males 16-21: 0; blacks over 16: 0; total blacks: 0; horses: 2; stud horses: 0; retail stores: 0; tavern license: 0.
Barren County Tax Book, 1800, part 1 - page: 7
FAMILY HISTORY LIBRARY film 7865

Goforth, Josiah,   Kentucky   Barren County
    Goforth, Josiah,   over 21 Male   **Color:** White
Acres of land: 0; County: 0; watercourse: 0; Entry: 0; Survey: 0; Patent: 0; white males over 21: 1; white males 16-21: 0; blacks over 16: 0; total blacks: 0; horses: 2; stud horses: 0; retail stores: 0; tavern license: 0.
Barren County Tax Book, 1800, part 1 - page: 7
FAMILY HISTORY LIBRARY film 7865

Gooden, Lewis,   Kentucky   Barren County
    Gooden, Lewis,   over 21 Male   **Color:** White
Acres of land: 200; Barren Co.; watercourse: Bluespring Creek; Entry: Lewis Gooden; Survey: same; Patent: 0; white males over 21: 1; white males 16-21: 0; blacks over 16: 0; total blacks: 0;

horses: 2; stud horses: 0; retail stores: 0; tavern license: 0.
Barren County Tax Book, 1800, part 1 - page: 6
FAMILY HISTORY LIBRARY film 7865

Gore, John,   Kentucky   Barren County
    Gore, John,   over 21 Male   **Color:** White
Acres of land: 200; Barren Co.; watercourse: Little Barren; Entry: John Gore; Survey: same; Patent: 0; white males over 21: 1; white males 16-21: 0; blacks over 16: 0; total blacks: 0; horses: 0; stud horses: 0; retail stores: 0; tavern license: 0.
Barren County Tax Book, 1800, part 1 - page: 6
FAMILY HISTORY LIBRARY film 7865

Green, John,   Kentucky   Barren County
    Green, John,   over 21 Male   **Color:** White
    Green,   16-21   Male   **Color:** White
Acres of land: 100; Barren Co.; watercourse: Bluespring Creek; Entry: John Green; Survey: same; Patent: 0; white males over 21: 1; white males 16-21: 1; blacks over 16: 0; total blacks: 0; horses: 4; stud horses: 0; retail stores: 0; tavern license: 0.
Barren County Tax Book, 1800, part 1 - page: 6
FAMILY HISTORY LIBRARY film 7865

Green, John,   Kentucky   Barren County
    Green, John,   Male
Acres of land: 100; Barren Co.; watercourse: Bluespring Creek; Entry: John Rotan; Survey: same; Patent: 0; white males over 21: 0; white males 16-21: 0; blacks over 16: 0; total blacks: 0; horses: 0; stud horses: 0; retail stores: 0; tavern license: 0.
Barren County Tax Book, 1800, part 1 - page: 6
FAMILY HISTORY LIBRARY film 7865

Green, William,   Kentucky   Barren County
    Green, William,   16-21   Male   **Color:** White
Acres of land: 146; Green Co.; watercourse: Green River; Entry: 0; Survey: 0; Patent: 0; white males over 21: 0; white males 16-21: 1; blacks over 16: 0; total blacks: 0; horses: 1; stud horses: 0; retail stores: 0; tavern license: 0.
Barren County Tax Book, 1800, part 1 - page: 6
FAMILY HISTORY LIBRARY film 7865

Grider, Christopher,   Kentucky   Barren County

Grider, Christopher,   over 21 Male
Color: White
Acres of land: 200; Barren Co.; watercourse: E F Big Barren; Entry: Christopher Grider; Survey: same; Patent: 0; white males over 21: 1; white males 16-21: 0; blacks over 16: 0; total blacks: 0; horses: 3; stud horses: 0; retail store: 0; tavern: 0.
Barren County Tax Book, 1800, part 1 - page: 6
FAMILY HISTORY LIBRARY film 7865
Grider, Jacob, Kentucky   Barren County
        Grider, Jacob,   over 21 Male   **Color:** White
Acres of land: 200; Barren Co.; watercourse: E. F. Big Barren; Entry: Jacob Grider; Survey: same; Patent: 0; white males over 21: 1; white males 16-21: 0; blacks over 16: 0; total blacks: 0; horses: 2; stud horses: 0; retail stores: 0; tavern license: 0.
Barren County Tax Book, 1800, part 1 - page: 6
FAMILY HISTORY LIBRARY film 7865
Griffin, Anthony,   Kentucky   Barren County
        Griffin, Anthony,   over 21 Male
        Color: White
Acres of land: 200; Barren Co.; watercourse: Skeggs Creek; Entry: Linsy? Mays; Survey: Anthony Griffin; Patent: 0; white males over 21: 1; white males 16-21: 0; blacks over 16: 0; total blacks: 0; horses: 4; stud horses: 0; retail store: 0; tavern: 0.
Barren County Tax Book, 1800, part 1 - page: 7
FAMILY HISTORY LIBRARY film 7865
Griffin, Richard, Kentucky   Barren County
        Griffin, Richard,   over 21 Male
        Color: White
Acres of land: 0; County: 0; watercourse: 0; Entry: 0; Survey: 0; Patent: 0; white males over 21: 1; white males 16-21: 0; blacks over 16: 0; total blacks: 0; horses: 3; stud horses: 0; retail stores: 0; tavern license: 0.
Barren County Tax Book, 1800, part 1 - page: 7
FAMILY HISTORY LIBRARY film 7865
Griggs, Daniel,   Kentucky   Barren County
        Griggs, Daniel, 16-21 Male   **Color:** White
Acres of land: 0; County: 0; watercourse: 0; Entry: 0; Survey: 0; Patent: 0; white males over 21: 0; white males 16-21: 1; blacks over 16: 0; total

blacks: 0; horses: 1; stud horses: 0; retail stores: 0; tavern license: 0.
Barren County Tax Book, 1800, part 1 - page: 6
FAMILY HISTORY LIBRARY film 7865
Griggs, John, Kentucky   Barren County?
        Griggs, John,   Male
The entry for land owned by Ferdinand Hamilton was in his name.
Barren County Tax Book, 1800, part 1 - page: 8
FAMILY HISTORY LIBRARY film 7865
Griggs, Joseph,   Kentucky   Barren County
        Griggs, Joseph, over 21 Male   **Color:** White
Acres of land: 0; County: 0; watercourse: 0; Entry: 0; Survey: 0; Patent: 0; white males over 21: 1; white males 16-21: 0; blacks over 16: 0; total blacks: 0; horses: 1; stud horses: 0; retail stores: 0; tavern license: 0.
Barren County Tax Book, 1800, part 1 - page: 6
FAMILY HISTORY LIBRARY film 7865
Griggs, Thomas,   Kentucky   Barren County
        Griggs, Thomas,   over 21 Male
        Color: White
Acres of land: 0; County: 0; watercourse: 0; Entry: 0; Survey: 0; Patent: 0; white males over 21: 1; white males 16-21: 0; blacks over 16: 0; total blacks: 0; horses: 2; stud horses: 0; retail stores: 0; tavern license: 0.
Barren County Tax Book, 1800, part 1 - page: 6
FAMILY HISTORY LIBRARY film 7865
Grimes, Jas, Kentucky   Barren County?
        Grimes, Jas,   Male
The entry for land owned by Moses Mitchel was in his name.
Barren County Tax Book, 1800, part 1 - page: 11
FAMILY HISTORY LIBRARY film 7865
Gum?, Jesse, Kentucky   Barren County
        Gum?, Jesse,   over 21 Male   **Color:** White
Acres of land: 200; Barren Co.; watercourse: Mill Creek; Entry: Jesse Gum?; Survey: same; Patent: 0; white males over 21: 1; white males 16-21: 0; blacks over 16: 0; total blacks: 0; horses: 3; stud horses: 0; retail stores: 0; tavern license: 0.
Barren County Tax Book, 1800, part 1 - page: 6
FAMILY HISTORY LIBRARY film 7865
Hagans, John, Kentucky   Barren County
        Hagans, John,   Male

Acres of land: 100; Green Co.; watercourse: E. F. Little Barren; Entry: John Hagans; Survey: same; Patent: 0; white males over 21: 0; white males 16-21: 0; blacks over 16: 0; total blacks: 0; horses: 0; stud horses: 0; retail stores: 0; tavern license: 0.
Barren County Tax Book, 1800, part 1 - page: 7
FAMILY HISTORY LIBRARY film 7865
Hagans, John, Kentucky   Barren County
 Hagans, John,   over 21 Male   **Color:** White
 Hagans,   over 21 Male   **Color:** White
Acres of land: 200; Barren Co.; watercourse: S. F. Little Barren; Entry: Samuel Hagans; Survey: same; Patent: 0; white males over 21: 2; white males 16-21: 0; blacks over 16: 0; total blacks: 0; horses: 4; stud horses: 0; retail store: 0; tavern: 0.
Barren County Tax Book, 1800, part 1 - page: 7
FAMILY HISTORY LIBRARY film 7865
Hagans, Samuel, Kentucky   Barren County?
 Hagans, Samuel,   Male
The entry for land owned by John Hagans was in his name.
Barren County Tax Book, 1800, part 1 - page: 7
FAMILY HISTORY LIBRARY film 7865
Hagans, William, Kentucky   Barren County
 Hagans, William,   over 21 Male
 Color: White
Acres of land: 200; Barren Co.; watercourse: S. F. Little Barren; Entry: Wm Hagans; Survey: same; Patent: 0; white males over 21: 1; white males 16-21: 0; blacks over 16: 0; total blacks: 0; horses: 4?; stud horses: 0; retail stores: 0; tavern license: 0.
Barren County Tax Book, 1800, part 1 - page: 7
FAMILY HISTORY LIBRARY film 7865
Hall, John, Kentucky   Barren County
 Hall, John,   over 21 Male   **Color:** White
Acres of land: 0; County: 0; watercourse: 0; Entry: 0; Survey: 0; Patent: 0; white males over 21: 1; white males 16-21: 0; blacks over 16: 0; total blacks: 0; horses: 2; stud horses: 0; retail stores: 0; tavern license: 0.
Barren County Tax Book, 1800, part 1 - page: 7
FAMILY HISTORY LIBRARY film 7865
Hall, Leonard, Kentucky   Barren County
 Hall, Leonard, over 21 Male   **Color:** White

Acres of land: 250; Barren Co.; watercourse: Beaver Creek; Entry: Lipscom Norvil?; Survey: same; Patent: same; white males over 21: 1; white males 16-21: 0; blacks over 16: 0; total blacks: 0; horses: 4; stud horses: 0; retail store: 0; tavern: 0.
Barren County Tax Book, 1800, part 1 - page: 7
FAMILY HISTORY LIBRARY film 7865
Hamilton, Abner, Kentucky   Barren County
 Hamilton, Abner,   over 21 Male
 Color: White
Acres of land: 200; Barren Co.; watercourse: Little Barren; Entry: 0; Survey: 0; Patent: 0; white males over 21: 1; white males 16-21: 0; blacks over 16: 0; total blacks: 0; horses: 12; stud horses: 0; retail stores: 0; tavern license: 0.
Barren County Tax Book, 1800, part 1 - page: 8
FAMILY HISTORY LIBRARY film 7865
Hamilton, Abner, Kentucky   Barren County
 Hamilton, Abner,   Male
Acres of land: 400; Barren Co.; watercourse: 0; Entry: 0; Survey: 0; Patent: 0; white males over 21: 0; white males 16-21: 0; blacks over 16: 0; total blacks: 0; horses: 0; stud horses: 0; retail stores: 0; tavern license: 0.
Barren County Tax Book, 1800, part 1 - page: 8
FAMILY HISTORY LIBRARY film 7865
Hamilton, Ferdinand, Kentucky   Barren County
 Hamilton, Ferdinand,   over 21 Male
 Color: White
 slave, over 16 Male   **Color:** Colored
Acres of land: 200; Barren Co.; watercourse: Peters Creek; Entry: John Griggs; Survey: same; Patent: 0; white males over 21: 1; white males 16-21: 0; blacks over 16: 1; total blacks: 3; horses: 3; stud horses: 0; retail stores: 0; tavern license: 0.
Barren County Tax Book, 1800, part 1 - page: 8
FAMILY HISTORY LIBRARY film 7865
Hamilton, Ferdinand, Kentucky   Barren County
 Hamilton, Ferdinand,   Male
Acres of land: 200; Barren Co.; watercourse: Peters Creek; Entry: Thos Fortner; Survey: same; Patent: 0; white males over 21: 0; white males 16-21: 0; blacks over 16: 0; total blacks: 0; horses: 0; stud horses: 0; retail stores: 0; tavern license: 0.
Barren County Tax Book, 1800, part 1 - page: 8
FAMILY HISTORY LIBRARY film 7865

Hamilton, John, Kentucky Barren County

        Hamilton, John, over 21 Male **Color:** White

        Hamilton, over 21 Male **Color:** White

Acres of land: 200; Barren Co.; watercourse: Skeggs Creek; Entry: John Hamilton; Survey: same; Patent: 0; white males over 21: 2; white males 16-21: 0; blacks over 16: 0; total blacks: 0; horses: 4; stud horses: 0; retail stores: 0; tavern license: 0.

Barren County Tax Book, 1800, part 1 - page: 8 FAMILY HISTORY LIBRARY film 7865

Hamilton, Robert, Kentucky Barren County

        Hamilton, Robert, over 21 Male **Color:** White

Acres of land: 0; County: 0; watercourse: 0; Entry: 0; Survey: 0; Patent: 0; white males over 21: 1; white males 16-21: 0; blacks over 16: 0; total blacks: 0; horses: 2; stud horses: 0; retail stores: 0; tavern license: 0.

Barren County Tax Book, 1800, part 1 - page: 8 FAMILY HISTORY LIBRARY film 7865

Handy, James, Kentucky Barren County

        Handy, James, over 21 Male **Color:** White

Acres of land: 200; Barren Co.; watercourse: Peters Creek; Entry: Jas Handy; Survey: same; Patent: 0; white males over 21: 1; white males 16-21: 0; blacks over 16: 0; total blacks: 0; horses: 0; stud horses: 0; retail stores: 0; tavern license: 0.

Barren County Tax Book, 1800, part 1 - page: 8 FAMILY HISTORY LIBRARY film 7865

Handy, William, Kentucky Barren County

        Handy, William, over 21 Male **Color:** White

        Handy, over 21 Male **Color:** White

        Handy, 16-21 Male **Color:** White

Acres of land: 166; Barren Co.; watercourse: Beaver Creek; Entry: Wm Handy; Survey: same; Patent: 0; white males over 21: 2; white males 16-21: 1; blacks over 16: 0; total blacks: 0; horses: 4; stud horses: 0; retail stores: 0; tavern license: 0.

Barren County Tax Book, 1800, part 1 - page: 8 FAMILY HISTORY LIBRARY film 7865

Handy, William, Kentucky Barren County

        Handy, William, Male

Acres of land: 100; Green Co.; watercourse: E F Little Barren; Entry: Wm Handy; Survey: same; Patent: 0; white males over 21: 0; white males 16-21: 0; blacks over 16: 0; total blacks: 0; horses: 0; stud horses: 0; retail stores: 0; tavern license: 0.

Barren County Tax Book, 1800, part 1 - page: 8 FAMILY HISTORY LIBRARY film 7865

Handy, William, Kentucky Barren County

        Handy, William, Male

Acres of land: 1000; Green Co.; watercourse: Russells Creek; Entry: Levi Walker; Survey: same; Patent: Abrm Eastridge; white males over 21: 0; white males 16-21: 0; blacks over 16: 0; total blacks: 0; horses: 0; stud horses: 0; retail store: 0; tavern: 0.

Barren County Tax Book, 1800, part 1 - page: 8 FAMILY HISTORY LIBRARY film 7865

Hardin, David, Kentucky Barren County

        Hardin, David, over 21 Male **Color:** White

        slave, over 16 Male **Color:** Colored

Acres of land: 100; Barren Co.; watercourse: E. F. Big Barren; Entry: Absalom Wood; Survey: same; Patent: 0; white males over 21: 1; white males 16-21: 0; blacks over 16: 1; total blacks: 1; horses: 3; stud horses: 0; retail stores: 0; tavern license: 0.

Barren County Tax Book, 1800, part 1 - page: 8 FAMILY HISTORY LIBRARY film 7865

Hardy, Curtis, Kentucky Barren County

        Hardy, Curtis, over 21 Male **Color:** White

        Hardy, over 21 Male **Color:** White

        Hardy, 16-21 Male **Color:** White

Acres of land: 200; Barren Co.; watercourse: Little Barren; Entry: Curtis Hardy; Survey: same; Patent: 0; white males over 21: 2; white males 16-21: 1; blacks over 16: 0; total blacks: 0; horses: 3; stud horses: 0; retail stores: 0; tavern license: 0.

Barren County Tax Book, 1800, part 1 - page: 8 FAMILY HISTORY LIBRARY film 7865

Hardy, George, Kentucky Barren County

        Hardy, George, over 21 Male **Color:** White

Acres of land: 200; Barren Co.; watercourse: Little Barren; Entry: George Hardy; Survey: same; Patent: 0; white males over 21: 1; white males 16-21: 0; blacks over 16: 0; total blacks: 0; horses: 0; stud horses: 0; retail stores: 0; tavern license: 0.
Barren County Tax Book, 1800, part 1 - page: 8
FAMILY HISTORY LIBRARY film 7865
Harlin, George, Kentucky Barren County
    Harlin, George, over 21 Male **Color:** White
Acres of land: 200; Barren Co.; watercourse: No Bob; Entry: Geo Harlin; Survey: same; Patent: 0; white males over 21: 1; white males 16-21: 0; blacks over 16: 0; total blacks: 0; horses: 6; stud horses: 0; retail stores: 0; tavern license: 0.
Barren County Tax Book, 1800, part 1 - page: 8
FAMILY HISTORY LIBRARY film 7865
Harlin, John, Junr Kentucky Barren County
    Harlin, John, Junr over 21 Male **Color:** White
Acres of land: 200; Barren Co.; watercourse: No Bob; Entry: Jacob Harlin; Survey: same; Patent: 0; white males over 21: 1; white males 16-21: 0; blacks over 16: 0; total blacks: 0; horses: 0; stud horses: 0; retail stores: 0; tavern license: 0.
Barren County Tax Book, 1800, part 1 - page: 8
FAMILY HISTORY LIBRARY film 7865
Harlin, John, senr Kentucky Barren County
    Harlin, John, senr over 21 Male **Color:** White
    Harlin, 16-21 Male **Color:** White
Acres of land: 200; Barren Co.; watercourse: No Bob; Entry: John Harlin senr; Survey: same; Patent: 0; white males over 21: 1; white males 16-21: 1; blacks over 16: 0; total blacks: 0; horses: 3; stud horses: 0; retail stores: 0; tavern license: 0.
Barren County Tax Book, 1800, part 1 - page: 8
FAMILY HISTORY LIBRARY film 7865
Harrard, James, Kentucky Barren County
    Harrard, James, over 21 Male **Color:** White
Acres of land: 0; County: 0; watercourse: 0; Entry: 0; Survey: 0; Patent: 0; white males over 21: 1; white males 16-21: 0; blacks over 16: 0; total blacks: 0; horses: 1; stud horses: 0; retail stores: 0; tavern license: 0.

Barren County Tax Book, 1800, part 1 - page: 7
FAMILY HISTORY LIBRARY film 7865
Harris, Richard, Kentucky Barren County
    Harris, Richard, over 21 Male **Color:** White
Acres of land: 200; Barren Co.; watercourse: Beaver Creek; Entry: Rih Harris; Survey: same; Patent: 0; white males over 21: 1; white males 16-21: 0; blacks over 16: 0; total blacks: 0; horses: 0; stud horses: 0; retail stores: 0; tavern license: 0.
Barren County Tax Book, 1800, part 1 - page: 7
FAMILY HISTORY LIBRARY film 7865
Hawkins, John, Kentucky Barren County?
    Hawkins, John, Male
The entry for land owned by Robert Hill was in his name.
Barren County Tax Book, 1800, part 1 - page: 7
FAMILY HISTORY LIBRARY film 7865
Hawkins, William, Kentucky Barren County
    Hawkins, William, over 21 Male **Color:** White
Acres of land: 0; County: 0, watercourse: 0; Entry: 0; Survey: 0; Patent: 0; white males over 21: 1; white males 16-21: 0; blacks over 16: 0; total blacks: 0; horses: 2; stud horses: 0; retail stores: 0; tavern license: 0.
Barren County Tax Book, 1800, part 1 - page: 8
FAMILY HISTORY LIBRARY film 7865
Haydon, Jerry, Kentucky Barren County
    Haydon, Jerry, over 21 Male **Color:** White
Acres of land: 0; County: 0; watercourse: 0; Entry: 0; Survey: 0; Patent: 0; white males over 21: 1; white males 16-21: 0; blacks over 16: 0; total blacks: 0; horses: 1; stud horses: 0; retail stores: 0; tavern license: 0.
Barren County Tax Book, 1800, part 1 - page: 8
FAMILY HISTORY LIBRARY film 7865
Henrick, Bird, Kentucky Barren County?
    Henrick, Bird, Male
The entry for land owned by Charles Allen was in his name.
Barren County Tax Book, 1800, part 1 - page: 1
FAMILY HISTORY LIBRARY film 7865
Hicklin, William, Kentucky Barren County

Hicklin, William,   over 21 Male
Color: White
Acres of land: 200; Barren Co.; watercourse: Big Barren; Entry: Wm Hicklin; Survey: same; Patent: 0; white males over 21: 1; white males 16-21: 0; blacks over 16: 0; total blacks: 0; horses: 5; stud horses: 0; retail stores: 0; tavern license: 0.
Barren County Tax Book, 1800, part 1 - page: 8
FAMILY HISTORY LIBRARY film 7865
Hicklin, William,   Kentucky   Barren County
        Hicklin, William,   Male
Acres of land: 200; Barren Co.; watercourse: E. F. Big Barren; Entry: 0; Survey: Wm Hicklin; Patent: 0; white males over 21: 0; white males 16-21: 0; blacks over 16: 0; total blacks: 0; horses: 0; stud horses: 0; retail stores: 0; tavern license: 0.
Barren County Tax Book, 1800, part 1 - page: 8
FAMILY HISTORY LIBRARY film 7865
Hill, Clement, Kentucky   Barren County
        Hill, Clement, over 21 Male   **Color:** White
Acres of land: 200; Barren Co.; watercourse: Little Barren; Entry: Clement Hill; Survey: same; Patent: 0; white males over 21: 1; white males 16-21: 0; blacks over 16: 0; total blacks: 0; horses: 5; stud horses: 0; retail stores: 0; tavern license: 0.
Barren County Tax Book, 1800, part 1 - page: 8
FAMILY HISTORY LIBRARY film 7865
Hill, Robert, Kentucky   Barren County
        Hill, Robert,   over 21 Male   **Color:** White
        slave, over 16 Male   **Color:** Colored
        slave, over 16 Male   **Color:** Colored
Acres of land: 200; Barren Co.; watercourse: Little Barren; Entry: Edmond Rogers; Survey: same; Patent: same; white males over 21: 1; white males 16-21: 0; blacks over 16: 2; total blacks: 4; horses: 8; stud horses: 0; retail stores: 0; tavern license: 0.
Barren County Tax Book, 1800, part 1 - page: 7
FAMILY HISTORY LIBRARY film 7865
Hill, Robert, Kentucky   Barren County
        Hill, Robert,   Male
Acres of land: 596?; County: 0; watercourse: Racoon Creek; Entry: John Hawkins; Survey: same; Patent: 0; white males over 21: 0; white males 16-21: 0; blacks over 16: 0; total blacks: 0; horses: 0; stud horses: 0; retail stores: 0; tavern license: 0.

Barren County Tax Book, 1800, part 1 - page: 7
FAMILY HISTORY LIBRARY film 7865
Hohimer or Hohuner, Henry, Kentucky
        Barren County
        Hohimer or Hohuner, Henry,   over   21   Male   **Color:** White
Acres of land: 0; County: 0; watercourse: 0; Entry: 0; Survey: 0; Patent: 0; white males over 21: 1; white males 16-21: 0; blacks over 16: 0; total blacks: 0; horses: 1; stud horses: 0; retail stores: 0; tavern license: 0.
Barren County Tax Book, 1800, part 1 - page: 7
FAMILY HISTORY LIBRARY film 7865
Hohuner or Hohimer, Henry, Kentucky
        Barren County
        Hohuner or Hohimer, Henry,   over   21   Male   **Color:** White
Acres of land: 0; County: 0; watercourse: 0; Entry: 0; Survey: 0; Patent: 0; white males over 21: 1; white males 16-21: 0; blacks over 16: 0; total blacks: 0; horses: 1; stud horses: 0; retail stores: 0; tavern license: 0.
Barren County Tax Book, 1800, part 1 - page: 7
FAMILY HISTORY LIBRARY film 7865
Holady, John A,   Kentucky   Barren County
        Holady, John A,   over 21 Male   **Color:** White
Acres of land: 200; Barren Co.; watercourse: E F Big Barren; Entry: James Doke; Survey: same; Patent: 0; white males over 21: 1; white males 16-21: 0; blacks over 16: 0; total blacks: 0; horses: 0; stud horses: 0; retail stores: 0; tavern license: 0.
Barren County Tax Book, 1800, part 1 - page: 7
FAMILY HISTORY LIBRARY film 7865
Holady, John A.,   Kentucky   Barren County
        Holady, John A.,   Male
Acres of land: 200; Barren Co.; watercourse: Beaver Creek; Entry: John A. Holady; Survey: same; Patent: 0; white males over 21: 0; white males 16-21: 0; blacks over 16: 0; total blacks: 0; horses: 0; stud horses: 0; retail stores: 0; tavern license: 0.
Barren County Tax Book, 1800, part 1 - page: 7
FAMILY HISTORY LIBRARY film 7865
Honnon, Abl, Kentucky   Barren County?
        Honnon, Abl,   Male
The entry for land owned by Daniel Curd was in his name.

Barren County Tax Book, 1800, part 1 - page: 3
FAMILY HISTORY LIBRARY film 7865
Houdeshilt, John, Kentucky Barren County
Houdeshilt, John, over 21 Male
Color: White
Acres of land: 200; Barren Co.; watercourse: Beaver Creek; Entry: Wm Rotan; Survey: same; Patent: 0; white males over 21: 1; white males 16-21: 0; blacks over 16: 0; total blacks: 0; horses: 4; stud horses: 0; retail stores: 0; tavern license: 0.
Barren County Tax Book, 1800, part 1 - page: 7
FAMILY HISTORY LIBRARY film 7865
Houttzelaw, Henry, Kentucky Barren County
Houttzelaw, Henry, over 21 Male
Color: White
Acres of land: 200?; Barren Co.; watercourse: White oak Creek; Entry: Henry Hottzelaw; Survey: same; Patent: 0; white males over 21: 1; white males 16-21: 0; blacks over 16: 0; total blacks: 0; horses: 5; stud horses: 0; retail store: 0; tavern: 0.
Barren County Tax Book, 1800, part 1 - page: 7
FAMILY HISTORY LIBRARY film 7865
How, John, Kentucky Barren County
How, John, over 21 Male **Color:** White
slave, over 16 Male **Color:** Colored
Acres of land: 200; Barren Co.; watercourse: Beaver Creek; Entry: McEntire; Survey: same; Patent: same; white males over 21: 1; white males 16-21: 0; blacks over 16: 1; total blacks: 1; horses: 3; stud horses: 0; retail stores: 0; tavern license: 0.
Barren County Tax Book, 1800, part 1 - page: 7
FAMILY HISTORY LIBRARY film 7865
Howel, James, Kentucky Barren County
Howel, James, over 21 Male **Color:** White
Acres of land: 200; Barren Co.; watercourse: Bluespring Creek; Entry: Jams Howel; Survey: same; Patent: 0; white males over 21: 1; white males 16-21: 0; blacks over 16: 0; total blacks: 0; horses: 3; stud horses: 0; retail stores: 0; tavern license: 0.
Barren County Tax Book, 1800, part 1 - page: 7
FAMILY HISTORY LIBRARY film 7865
Huffman, Ambrose, Kentucky Barren County
Huffman, Ambrose, over 21 Male
Color: White
Acres of land: 200; Barren Co.; watercourse: Big Barren?; Entry: Ambrose Houghman; Survey: same; Patent: 0; white males over 21: 1; white males 16-21: 0; blacks over 16: 0; total blacks: 0; horses: 3; stud horses: 0; retail stores: 0; tavern license: 0.
Barren County Tax Book, 1800, part 1 - page: 8
FAMILY HISTORY LIBRARY film 7865
Hunter, Wm, Kentucky Barren County?
Hunter, Wm, Male
The entry for land owned by Nathan Breed was in his name.
Barren County Tax Book, 1800, part 1 - page: 2
FAMILY HISTORY LIBRARY film 7865
Huston, Isaac, Kentucky Barren County
Huston, Isaac, over 21 Male **Color:** White
Acres of land: 0; County: 0; watercourse: 0; Entry: 0; Survey: 0; Patent: 0; white males over 21: 1; white males 16-21: 0; blacks over 16: 0; total blacks: 0; horses: 5; stud horses: 0; retail stores: 0; tavern license: 0.
Barren County Tax Book, 1800, part 1 - page: 7
FAMILY HISTORY LIBRARY film 7865
Ingraham, P., Kentucky Barren County?
Ingraham, P., Male
The entry for land owned by Edmond Rogers was in the names of P. Ingraham and A Cray . . . .
Barren County Tax Book, 1800, part 1 - page: 13
FAMILY HISTORY LIBRARY film 7865
James?, Joseph?, Kentucky Barren County
James?, Joseph?, over 21 Male
Color: White
Acres of land: 100; Cumberland? Co.; watercourse: ?; Entry: Joseph? James?; Survey: same; Patent: 0; white males over 21: 1; white males 16-21: 0; blacks over 16: 0; total blacks: 0; horses: ?; stud horses: 0; retail stores: 0; tavern license: 0.
Barren County Tax Book, 1800, part 1 - page: 8
FAMILY HISTORY LIBRARY film 7865
Jenkins, Jobe, Kentucky Barren County
Jenkins, Jobe, over 21 Male **Color:** White
Jenkins, over 21 Male **Color:** White
Acres of land: 0; County: 0; watercourse: 0; Entry: 0; Survey: 0; Patent: 0; white males over 21: 2; white males 16-21: 0; blacks over 16: 0; total

blacks: 0; horses: 1; stud horses: 0; retail stores: 0; tavern license: 0.
Barren County Tax Book, 1800, part 1 - page: 8
FAMILY HISTORY LIBRARY film 7865
Jenkins, William, Kentucky Barren County
Jenkins, William, Male
Acres of land: 500; Mason Co.; watercourse: Big Sandy; Entry: Wm Jenkins; Survey: same; Patent: 0; white males over 21: 0; white males 16-21: 0; blacks over 16: 0; total blacks: 0; horses: 0; stud horses: 0; retail stores: 0; tavern license: 0.
Barren County Tax Book, 1800, part 1 - page: 9
FAMILY HISTORY LIBRARY film 7865
Jenkins, William, senr Kentucky Barren County
Jenkins, William, senr Male
Acres of land: 295; Montgomery Co.; watercourse: Grass Lick; Entry: Wm Jenkins; Survey: same; Patent: same; white males over 21: 0; white males 16-21: 0; blacks over 16: 0; total blacks: 0; horses: 0; stud horses: 0; retail stores: 0; tavern license: 0.
Barren County Tax Book, 1800, part 1 - page: 9
FAMILY HISTORY LIBRARY film 7865
Jenkins, William, senr Kentucky Barren County
Jenkins, William, senr over 21 Male **Color:** White
Jenkins, 16-21 Male **Color:** White
Acres of land: 200; Barren Co.; watercourse: Skeggs Creek; Entry: Edwin Summers; Survey: Wm Jenkins; Patent: 0; white males over 21: 1; white males 16-21: 1; blacks over 16: 0; total blacks: 0; horses: 4; stud horses: 0; retail store: 0; tavern: 0.
Barren County Tax Book, 1800, part 1 - page: 9
FAMILY HISTORY LIBRARY film 7865
Jerot, John, Kentucky Barren County?
Jerot, John, Male
The entry for land owned by William Anderson was in his name.
Barren County Tax Book, 1800, part 1 - page: 1
FAMILY HISTORY LIBRARY film 7865
Jewell, William, Kentucky Barren County
Jewell, William, over 21 Male **Color:** White
Acres of land: 0; County: 0; watercourse: 0; Entry: 0; Survey: 0; Patent: 0; white males over 21: 1;

white males 16-21: 0; blacks over 16: 0; total blacks: 0; horses: 5; stud horses: 1; retail stores: 0; tavern license: 0.
Barren County Tax Book, 1800, part 1 - page: 8
FAMILY HISTORY LIBRARY film 7865
Jimmerson, Garrard, Kentucky Barren County
Jimmerson, Garrard, over 21 Male **Color:** White
Acres of land: 0; County: 0; watercourse: 0; Entry: 0; Survey: 0; Patent: 0; white males over 21: 1; white males 16-21: 0; blacks over 16: 0; total blacks: 0; horses: 2; stud horses: 0; retail stores: 0; tavern license: 0.
Barren County Tax Book, 1800, part 1 - page: 8
FAMILY HISTORY LIBRARY film 7865
Jobe, David, Kentucky Barren County
Jobe, David, over 21 Male **Color:** White
Acres of land: 200; Barren Co.; watercourse: Coles Creek; Entry: David Jobe; Survey: same; Patent: 0; white males over 21: 1; white males 16-21: 0; blacks over 16: 0; total blacks: 0; horses: 3; stud horses: 0; retail stores: 0; tavern license: 0.
Barren County Tax Book, 1800, part 1 - page: 9
FAMILY HISTORY LIBRARY film 7865
Jobe, Enoch, Kentucky Barren County
Jobe, Enoch, over 21 Male **Color:** White
Acres of land: 150; Barren Co.; watercourse: Mill Creek; Entry: Enoch Jobe; Survey: same; Patent: 0; white males over 21: 1; white males 16-21: 0; blacks over 16: 0; total blacks: 0; horses: 1; stud horses: 0; retail stores: 0; tavern license: 0.
Barren County Tax Book, 1800, part 1 - page: 9
FAMILY HISTORY LIBRARY film 7865
Jobe, Jesse, Kentucky Barren County
Jobe, Jesse, over 21 Male **Color:** White
Acres of land: 200; Barren Co.; watercourse: Coles Creek; Entry: Jesse Jobe; Survey: same; Patent: 0; white males over 21: 1; white males 16-21: 0; blacks over 16: 0; total blacks: 0; horses: 1; stud horses: 0; retail stores: 0; tavern license: 0.
Barren County Tax Book, 1800, part 1 - page: 9
FAMILY HISTORY LIBRARY film 7865
Johnson, James, Kentucky Barren County
Johnson, James, over 21 Male **Color:** White

Acres of land: 200; Barren Co.; watercourse: Poters Creek; Entry: Robt Bernsides; Survey: James Johnson; Patent: 0; white males over 21: 1; white males 16-21: 0; blacks over 16: 0; total blacks: 1; horses: 2; stud horses: 0; retail store: 0; tavern: 0.
Barren County Tax Book, 1800, part 1 - page: 9
FAMILY HISTORY LIBRARY film 7865

Johnson, John, Kentucky Barren County

    Johnson, John, over 21 Male **Color:** White

Acres of land: 0; County: 0; watercourse: 0; Entry: 0; Survey: 0; Patent: 0; white males over 21: 1; white males 16-21: 0; blacks over 16: 0; total blacks: 0; horses: 3; stud horses: 0; retail stores: 0; tavern license: 0.
Barren County Tax Book, 1800, part 1 - page: 9
FAMILY HISTORY LIBRARY film 7865

Johnson, Zachariah, Kentucky Barren County

    Johnson, Zachariah, over 21 Male **Color:** White

Acres of land: 0; County: 0; watercourse: 0; Entry: 0; Survey: 0; Patent: 0; white males over 21: 1; white males 16-21: 0; blacks over 16: 0; total blacks: 0; horses: 4; stud horses: 0; retail stores: 0; tavern license: 0.
Barren County Tax Book, 1800, part 1 - page: 8
FAMILY HISTORY LIBRARY film 7865

Jolliff, James, Kentucky Barren County

    Jolliff, James, over 21 Male **Color:** White

Acres of land: 150; County: 0; watercourse: 0; Entry: 0; Survey: 0; Patent: 0; white males over 21: 1; white males 16-21: 0; blacks over 16: 0; total blacks: 0; horses: 7; stud horses: 0; retail stores: 0; tavern license: 0.
Barren County Tax Book, 1800, part 1 - page: 8
FAMILY HISTORY LIBRARY film 7865

Jones, John, Kentucky Barren County

    Jones, John, over 21 Male **Color:** White

Acres of land: 0; County: 0; watercourse: 0; Entry: 0; Survey: 0; Patent: 0; white males over 21: 1; white males 16-21: 0; blacks over 16: 0; total blacks: 0; horses: 1; stud horses: 0; retail stores: 0; tavern license: 0.
Barren County Tax Book, 1800, part 1 - page: 8
FAMILY HISTORY LIBRARY film 7865

Jones, Joseph, Kentucky Barren County

    Jones, Joseph, Male

Acres of land: 100; Cumberland Co.; watercourse: Little Renicks? Creek; Entry: 0; Survey: Henry Renick; Patent: 0; white males over 21: 0; white males 16-21: 0; blacks over 16: 0; total blacks: 0; horses: 0; stud horses: 0; tavern: 0.
Barren County Tax Book, 1800, part 1 - page: 8
FAMILY HISTORY LIBRARY film 7865

Jones, Joseph, Kentucky Barren County

    Jones, Joseph, over 21 Male **Color:** White
    Jones, 16-21 Male **Color:** White
    slave, over 16 Male **Color:** Colored

Acres of land: 100; Cumberland Co.; watercourse: Little Renicks? Creek; Entry: Joseph Jones; Survey: same; Patent: 0; white males over 21: 1; white males 16-21: 1; blacks over 16: 1; total blacks: 1; horses: 5; stud horses: 0; retail store: 0; tavern: 0.
Barren County Tax Book, 1800, part 1 - page: 8
FAMILY HISTORY LIBRARY film 7865

Kays, George, Kentucky Barren County

    Kays, George, over 21 Male **Color:** White
    Kays, 16-21 Male **Color:** White

Acres of land: 200; Barren Co.; watercourse: Skeggs Creek; Entry: Geo Kays; Survey: same; Patent: 0; white males over 21: 1; white males 16-21: 1; blacks over 16: 0; total blacks: 0; horses: 4; stud horses: 0; retail stores: 0; tavern license: 0.
Barren County Tax Book, 1800, part 1 - page: 9
FAMILY HISTORY LIBRARY film 7865

Kelley, John, Kentucky Barren County

    Kelley, John, over 21 Male **Color:** White

Acres of land: 0; County: 0; watercourse: 0; Entry: 0; Survey: 0; Patent: 0; white males over 21: 1; white males 16-21: 0; blacks over 16: 0; total blacks: 0; horses: 0; stud horses: 0; retail stores: 0; tavern license: 0.
Barren County Tax Book, 1800, part 1 - page: 9
FAMILY HISTORY LIBRARY film 7865

Kendall, Frances, Kentucky Barren County

    Kendall, Frances, over 21 Male **Color:** White

Acres of land: 0; County: 0; watercourse: 0; Entry: 0; Survey: 0; Patent: 0; white males over 21: 1; white males 16-21: 0; blacks over 16: 0; total

blacks: 0; horses: 1; stud horses: 0; retail stores: 0; tavern license: 0.
Barren County Tax Book, 1800, part 1 - page: 9
FAMILY HISTORY LIBRARY film 7865
Kerby, Robert, Kentucky Barren County
Kerby, Robert, over 21 Male **Color:** White
Acres of land: 100; Barren Co.; watercourse: Mill Creek; Entry: Robt Kerby; Survey: same; Patent: 0; white males over 21: 1; white males 16-21: 0; blacks over 16: 0; total blacks: 0; horses: 1; stud horses: 0; retail stores: 0; tavern license: 0.
Barren County Tax Book, 1800, part 1 - page: 9
FAMILY HISTORY LIBRARY film 7865
Kerkham, Henry, Kentucky Barren County
Kerkham, Henry, over 21 Male **Color:** White
Acres of land: 0; County: 0; watercourse: 0; Entry: 0; Survey: 0; Patent: 0; white males over 21: 1; white males 16-21: 0; blacks over 16: 0; total blacks: 0; horses: 5; stud horses: 0; retail stores: 0; tavern license: 0.
Barren County Tax Book, 1800, part 1 - page: 9
FAMILY HISTORY LIBRARY film 7865
Kerkham, Michael, Kentucky Barren County
Kerkham, Michael, over 21 Male **Color:** White
Kerkham, over 21 Male **Color:** White
Kerkham, 16-21 Male **Color:** White
slave, over 16 Male **Color:** Colored
slave, over 16 Male **Color:** Colored
Acres of land: 0; County: 0; watercourse: 0; Entry: 0; Survey: 0; Patent: 0; white males over 21: 2; white males 16-21: 1; blacks over 16: 2; total blacks: 3; horses: 16; stud horses: 0; retail stores: 0; tavern license: 0.
Barren County Tax Book, 1800, part 1 - page: 9
FAMILY HISTORY LIBRARY film 7865
Kerr, Nathaniel, Kentucky Barren County
Kerr, Nathaniel, over 21 Male **Color:** White
Kerr, 16-21 Male **Color:** White
Acres of land: 0; County: 0; watercourse: 0; Entry: 0; Survey: 0; Patent: 0; white males over 21: 1;
white males 16-21: 1; blacks over 16: 0; total blacks: 0; horses: 4; stud horses: 0; retail stores: 0; tavern license: 0.
Barren County Tax Book, 1800, part 1 - page: 9
FAMILY HISTORY LIBRARY film 7865
King, Benjamin, Kentucky Barren County
King, Benjamin, over 21 Male **Color:** White
Acres of land: 0; County: 0; watercourse: 0; Entry: 0; Survey: 0; Patent: 0; white males over 21: 1; white males 16-21: 0; blacks over 16: 0; total blacks: 0; horses: 1; stud horses: 0; retail stores: 0; tavern license: 0.
Barren County Tax Book, 1800, part 1 - page: 9
FAMILY HISTORY LIBRARY film 7865
King, Benjamin, Kentucky Barren County?
King, Benjamin, Male
The entry for land owned by Roderik Rollins was in his name.
Barren County Tax Book, 1800, part 1 - page: 12
FAMILY HISTORY LIBRARY film 7865
King, John, Kentucky Barren County
King, John, over 21 Male **Color:** White
slave, over 16 Male **Color:** Colored
Acres of land: 200; Barren Co.; watercourse: Beaver? Creek; Entry: John King; Survey: same; Patent: 0; white males over 21: 1; white males 16-21: 0; blacks over 16: 1; total blacks: 3; horses: 6; stud horses: 0; retail stores: 0; tavern license: 0.
Barren County Tax Book, 1800, part 1 - page: 9
FAMILY HISTORY LIBRARY film 7865
Lamb, Wm, Kentucky Barren County?
Lamb, Wm, Male
The entry for land owned by Andrew Beard was in his name.
Barren County Tax Book, 1800, part 1 - page: 2
FAMILY HISTORY LIBRARY film 7865
Lanham, William, Kentucky Barren County
Lanham, William, over 21 Male **Color:** White
Acres of land: 0; County: 0; watercourse: 0; Entry: 0; Survey: 0; Patent: 0; white males over 21: 1; white males 16-21: 0; blacks over 16: 0; total blacks: 0; horses: 1; stud horses: 0; retail stores: 0; tavern license: 0.

Barren County Tax Book, 1800, part 1 - page: 9
FAMILY HISTORY LIBRARY film 7865
Lasswell, William,   Kentucky   Barren County
        Lasswell, William,   over 21 Male
        Color: White
Acres of land: 200; Barren Co.; watercourse: S F Little Barren; Entry: Wm Lasswell; Survey: same; Patent: 0; white males over 21: 1; white males 16-21: 0; blacks over 16: 0; total blacks: 0; horses: 5; stud horses: 0; retail stores: 0; tavern license: 0.
Barren County Tax Book, 1800, part 1 - page: 9
FAMILY HISTORY LIBRARY film 7865
Latimore, Frances,   Kentucky   Barren County
        Latimore, Frances,   Male
Acres of land: 150; Barren Co.; watercourse: Beaver Creek; Entry: Thos Smart; Survey: same; Patent: 0; white males over 21: 0; white males 16-21: 0; blacks over 16: 0; total blacks: 0; horses: 0; stud horses: 0; retail stores: 0; tavern license: 0.
Barren County Tax Book, 1800, part 1 - page: 9
FAMILY HISTORY LIBRARY film 7865
Latimore, Frances,   Kentucky   Barren County
        Latimore, Frances,   over 21 Male
        Color: White
        slave, over 16 Male   **Color:** Colored
        slave, over 16 Male   **Color:** Colored
Acres of land: 200; Barren Co.; watercourse: Beaver Creek; Entry: Frances Latimore; Survey: same; Patent: 0; white males over 21: 1; white males 16-21: 0; blacks over 16: 2; total blacks: 6; horses: 5; stud horses: 0; retail stores: 0; tavern license: 0.
Barren County Tax Book, 1800, part 1 - page: 9
FAMILY HISTORY LIBRARY film 7865
Layne?, Wm M,   Kentucky   Barren County?
        Layne?, Wm M,   Male
The entry for land owned by Nathan Breed was in his name.
Barren County Tax Book, 1800, part 1 - page: 2
FAMILY HISTORY LIBRARY film 7865
Lee, John,   Kentucky   Barren County
        Lee, John,   16-21 Male   **Color:** White
Acres of land: 0; County: 0; watercourse: 0; Entry: 0; Survey: 0; Patent: 0; white males over 21: 0; white males 16-21: 1; blacks over 16: 0; total blacks: 0; horses: 1; stud horses: 0; retail stores: 0; tavern license: 0.
Barren County Tax Book, 1800, part 1 - page: 9
FAMILY HISTORY LIBRARY film 7865
Lerty, John,   Kentucky   Barren County?
        Lerty, John,   Male
The entry for land owned by William Courts was in his name.
Barren County Tax Book, 1800, part 1 - page: 4
FAMILY HISTORY LIBRARY film 7865
Lerty, John,   Kentucky   Barren County?
        Lerty, John,   Male
The entry for land owned by John Courts was in his name.
Barren County Tax Book, 1800, part 1 - page: 4
FAMILY HISTORY LIBRARY film 7865
Lettch, James, Kentucky   Barren County
        Lettch, James, over 21 Male   **Color:** White
Acres of land: 0; County: 0; watercourse: 0; Entry: 0; Survey: 0; Patent: 0; white males over 21: 1; white males 16-21: 0; blacks over 16: 0; total blacks: 0; horses: 4; stud horses: 0; retail stores: 0; tavern license: 0.
Barren County Tax Book, 1800, part 1 - page: 9
FAMILY HISTORY LIBRARY film 7865
Lloyd, Thomas,   Kentucky   Barren County
        Lloyd, Thomas,   over 21 Male
        Color: White
Acres of land: 200; Barren Co.; watercourse: Fallen Timber; Entry: Thos Lloyd; Survey: same; Patent: 0; white males over 21: 1; white males 16-21: 0; blacks over 16: 0; total blacks: 0; horses: 0; stud horses: 0; retail stores: 0; tavern license: 0.
Barren County Tax Book, 1800, part 1 - page: 9
FAMILY HISTORY LIBRARY film 7865
Logan, William,   Kentucky   Barren County
        Logan, William,   over 21 Male
        Color: White
Acres of land: 0; County: 0; watercourse: 0; Entry: 0; Survey: 0; Patent: 0; white males over 21: 1; white males 16-21: 0; blacks over 16: 0; total blacks: 0; horses: 1; stud horses: 0; retail stores: 0; tavern license: 0.
Barren County Tax Book, 1800, part 1 - page: 9
FAMILY HISTORY LIBRARY film 7865
Logue, William,   Kentucky   Barren County

Logue, William, over 21 Male
Color: White
Acres of land: 0; County: 0; watercourse: 0; Entry: 0; Survey: 0; Patent: 0; white males over 21: 1; white males 16-21: 0; blacks over 16: 0; total blacks: 0; horses: 3; stud horses: 0; retail stores: 0; tavern license: 0.
Barren County Tax Book, 1800, part 1 - page: 9
FAMILY HISTORY LIBRARY film 7865
Long, Christopher, Kentucky Barren County
Long, Christopher, over 21 Male
Color: White
Acres of land: 0; County: 0; watercourse: 0; Entry: 0; Survey: 0; Patent: 0; white males over 21: 1; white males 16-21: 0; blacks over 16: 0; total blacks: 0; horses: 1; stud horses: 0; retail stores: 0; tavern license: 0.
Barren County Tax Book, 1800, part 1 - page: 9
FAMILY HISTORY LIBRARY film 7865
Lowry, Alexander, Kentucky Barren County
Lowry, Alexander, over 21 Male
Color: White
Acres of land: 150?; Barren Co.; watercourse: Line Creek; Entry: Jesse Russell; Survey: same; Patent: 0; white males over 21: 1; white males 16-21: 0; blacks over 16: 0; total blacks: 0; horses: 1; stud horses: 0; retail stores: 0; tavern license: 0.
Barren County Tax Book, 1800, part 1 - page: 9
FAMILY HISTORY LIBRARY film 7865
Mackay, William, Kentucky Barren County
Mackay, William, over 21 Male
Color: White
Mackay, 16-21 Male **Color:** White
slave, over 16 Male **Color:** Colored
Acres of land: 200; Barren Co.; watercourse: Little Barren; Entry: Wm Mackay; Survey: same; Patent: same; white males over 21: 1; white males 16-21: 1; blacks over 16: 1; total blacks: 4; horses: 7; stud horses: 0; retail stores: 0; tavern license: 0.
Barren County Tax Book, 1800, part 1 - page: 10
FAMILY HISTORY LIBRARY film 7865
Mackay, William, Kentucky Barren County
Mackay, William, Male
Acres of land: 200; Barren Co.; watercourse: Beaver Creek; Entry: Wm Mackay; Survey: same;
Patent: 0; white males over 21: 0; white males 16-21: 0; blacks over 16: 0; total blacks: 0; horses: 0; stud horses: 0; retail stores: 0; tavern license: 0.
Barren County Tax Book, 1800, part 1 - page: 10
FAMILY HISTORY LIBRARY film 7865
Mackay, William, Kentucky Barren County
Mackay, William, Male
Acres of land: 200; Barren Co.; watercourse: Beaver Creek; Entry: Wm Mackay; Survey: same; Patent: same; white males over 21: 0; white males 16-21: 0; blacks over 16: 0; total blacks: 0; horses: 0; stud horses: 0; retail stores: 0; tavern license: 0.
Barren County Tax Book, 1800, part 1 - page: 10
FAMILY HISTORY LIBRARY film 7865
Malone, Wynn, Kentucky Barren County
Malone, Wynn, over 21 Male **Color:** White
Malone, 16-21 Male **Color:** White
slave, over 16 Male **Color:** Colored
Acres of land: 0; County: 0; watercourse: 0; Entry: 0; Survey: 0; Patent: 0; white males over 21: 1; white males 16-21: 1; blacks over 16: 1; total blacks: 3; horses: 2; stud horses: 0; retail stores: 0; tavern license: 0.
Barren County Tax Book, 1800, part 1 - page: 10
FAMILY HISTORY LIBRARY film 7865
Marrs, Samuel, Kentucky Barren County
Marrs, Samuel, over 21 Male **Color:** White
Acres of land: 200; Barren Co.; watercourse: Mill Creek; Entry: Saml Marrs; Survey: same; Patent: 0; white males over 21: 1; white males 16-21: 0; blacks over 16: 0; total blacks: 0; horses: 2; stud horses: 0; retail stores: 0; tavern license: 0.
Barren County Tax Book, 1800, part 1 - page: 10
FAMILY HISTORY LIBRARY film 7865
Marshall, Hugh, Kentucky Barren County
Marshall, Hugh, over 21 Male
Color: White
Acres: 200; County: Barren; watercourse: Peters Creek; Entry: Walter Bernsides; Survey: same; Patent: 0; white males over 21: 1; white males 16-21: 0; blacks over 16: 0; total blacks: 1; horses: 3; stud horses: 0; retail store: 0; tavern lic.: 0.

Barren County Tax Book, 1800, part 1 - page: 11
FAMILY HISTORY LIBRARY film 7865
Marshall, Thos, Kentucky Barren
County?
    Marshall, Thos, Male
The entry for land owned by John Robinson was in
his name.
Barren County Tax Book, 1800, part 1 - page: 13
FAMILY HISTORY LIBRARY film 7865
Martin, Jas, Kentucky Barren County?
    Martin, Jas, Male
The entry for land owned by Joseph Martin was in
his name.
Barren County Tax Book, 1800, part 1 - page: 11
FAMILY HISTORY LIBRARY film 7865
Martin, John, Kentucky Barren County
    Martin, John, over 21 Male **Color:**
    White
    slave, over 16 Male **Color:** Colored
Acres: 200; County: Barren; watercourse: Peters
Creek; Entry: John Martin; Survey: same; Patent:
0; white males over 21: 1; white males 16-21: 0;
blacks over 16: 1; total blacks: 2; horses: 10; stud
horses: 0; retail store: 0; tavern lic.: 0.
Barren County Tax Book, 1800, part 1 - page: 11
FAMILY HISTORY LIBRARY film 7865
Martin, Joseph, Kentucky Barren
County
    Martin, Joseph, over 21 Male **Color:**
    White
    slave, over 16 Male **Color:** Colored
    slave, over 16 Male **Color:** Colored
Acres: 200; County: Barren; watercourse: Skeggs
Creek; Entry: Wm Perkins; Survey: same; Patent:
0; white males over 21: 1; white males 16-21: 0;
blacks over 16: 2; total blacks: 5; horses: 3?; stud
horses: 0; retail store: 0; tavern lic.: 0.
Barren County Tax Book, 1800, part 1 - page: 11
FAMILY HISTORY LIBRARY film 7865
Martin, Joseph, Kentucky Barren
County
    Martin, Joseph, over 21 Male **Color:**
    White
Acres: 200; County: Barren; watercourse: Peters
Creek; Entry: Joseph Martin; Survey: same; Patent:
0; white males over 21: 1; white males 16-21: 0;
blacks over 16: 0; total blacks: 0; horses: 2; stud
horses: 0; retail store: 0; tavern lic.: 0.
Barren County Tax Book, 1800, part 1 - page: 11
FAMILY HISTORY LIBRARY film 7865

Martin, Joseph, Kentucky Barren
County
    Martin, Joseph, Male
Acres: 200; County: Barren; watercourse: Peters
Creek; Entry: Jas Martin; Survey: 0; Patent: 0;
white males over 21: 0; white males 16-21: 0;
blacks over 16: 0, total blacks: 0; horses: 0; stud
horses: 0; retail store: 0; tavern lic.: 0.
Barren County Tax Book, 1800, part 1 - page: 11
FAMILY HISTORY LIBRARY film 7865
Martin, William, Kentucky Barren
County
    Martin, William, over 21 Male
    Color: White
    Martin, over 21 Male **Color:** White
    slave, over 16 Male **Color:** Colored
    slave, over 16 Male **Color:** Colored
Acres: 1000; County: Barren; watercourse: Peters
Creek; Entry: Wm Cammel; Survey: same; Patent:
Carrolson?; white males over 21: 2; white males
16-21: 0; blacks over 16: 2; total blacks: 7; horses:
6; stud horses: 1; retail store: 0; tavern lic.: 0.
Barren County Tax Book, 1800, part 1 - page: 11
FAMILY HISTORY LIBRARY film 7865
Martin, William, Kentucky Barren
County
    Martin, William, Male
Acres: 200; County: Barren; watercourse: Peters
Creek; Entry: Wm Martin; Survey: same; Patent:
0; white males over 21: 0; white males 16-21: 0;
blacks over 16: 0; total blacks: 0; horses: 0; stud
horses: 0; retail store: 0; tavern lic.: 0.
Barren County Tax Book, 1800, part 1 - page: 11
FAMILY HISTORY LIBRARY film 7865
Mathews, J, Kentucky Barren County?
    Mathews, J, Male
The patent for land owned by Moses Mitchel was
in his name and that of M. Mitchel.
Barren County Tax Book, 1800, part 1 - page: 11
FAMILY HISTORY LIBRARY film 7865
Matthews, William, Kentucky Barren
County?
    Matthews, William, Male
The entry for land owned by Ezekiel Downy was
in his name.
Barren County Tax Book, 1800, part 1 - page: 5
FAMILY HISTORY LIBRARY film 7865
Mayfield, Geddeon, Kentucky Barren
County

Mayfield, Geddeon,   over 21 Male
Color: White
Acres of land: 200; Barren Co.; watercourse: Mill Creek; Entry: Jno Scott; Survey: same; Patent: 0; white males over 21: 1; white males 16-21: 0; blacks over 16: 0; total blacks: 0; horses: 2; stud horses: 0; retail stores: 0; tavern license: 0.
Barren County Tax Book, 1800, part 1 - page: 10
FAMILY HISTORY LIBRARY film 7865
Mayfield, Geddeon,   Kentucky   Barren County
        Mayfield, Geddeon,   Male
Acres of land: 200; Barren Co.; watercourse: Mill Creek; Entry: Geddeon Mayfield; Survey: same; Patent: 0; white males over 21: 0; white males 16-21: 0; blacks over 16: 0; total blacks: 0; horses: 0; stud horses: 0; retail stores: 0; tavern license: 0.
Barren County Tax Book, 1800, part 1 - page: 10
FAMILY HISTORY LIBRARY film 7865
Mays, Linsy?, Kentucky   Barren County?
        Mays, Linsy?,   Male
The entry for land owned by Anthony Griffin was in his name.
Barren County Tax Book, 1800, part 1 - page: 7
FAMILY HISTORY LIBRARY film 7865
McCalley?, John?,   Kentucky   Barren County
        McCalley?, John?,   over 21 Male
        Color: White
Acres of land: 0; County: 0; watercourse: 0; Entry: 0; Survey: 0; Patent: 0; white males over 21: 1; white males 16-21: 0; blacks over 16: 0; total blacks: 0; horses: 2?; stud horses: 0; retail stores: 0; tavern license: 0.
Barren County Tax Book, 1800, part 1 - page: 10
FAMILY HISTORY LIBRARY film 7865
McCartey, Elisha,   Kentucky   Barren County
        McCartey, Elisha,   Male
Acres: 0; County: 0; watercourse: 0; Entry: 0; Survey: 0; Patent: 0; white males over 21: 1; white males 16-21: 0; blacks over 16: 0; total blacks: 0; horses: 1; stud horses: 0; retail store: 0; tavern lic.: 0.
Barren County Tax Book, 1800, part 1 - page: 11
FAMILY HISTORY LIBRARY film 7865
McClain, James,   Kentucky   Barren County
        McClain, James,   over 21 Male
        Color: White

Acres of land: 200; Barren Co.; watercourse: Bluespring Creek; Entry: Jas McClain; Survey: same; Patent: 0; white males over 21: 1; white males 16-21: 0; blacks over 16: 0; total blacks: 0; horses: 1; stud horses: 0; retail stores: 0; tavern license: 0.
Barren County Tax Book, 1800, part 1 - page: 10
FAMILY HISTORY LIBRARY film 7865
McClain, Thomas,   Kentucky   Barren County
        McClain, Thomas,   over 21 Male
        Color: White
Acres: 200; County: Barren; watercourse: Bluespring Creek; Entry: Thos McClain; Survey: same; Patent: 0; white males over 21: 1; white males 16-21: 0; blacks over 16: 0; total blacks: 0; horses: 2; stud horses: 0; retail store: 0; tavern lic.: 0.
Barren County Tax Book, 1800, part 1 - page: 11
FAMILY HISTORY LIBRARY film 7865
McCoy, Alexander,   Kentucky   Barren County
        McCoy, Alexander,   over 21 Male
        Color: White
        McCoy,   16-21 Male   **Color:** White
Acres of land: 150; Barren Co.; watercourse: Beaver Creek; Entry: Alex McCoy; Survey: same; Patent: 0; white males over 21: 1; white males 16-21: 1; blacks over 16: 0; total blacks: 0; horses: 4; stud horses: 0; retail stores: 0; tavern license: 0.
Barren County Tax Book, 1800, part 1 - page: 10
FAMILY HISTORY LIBRARY film 7865
McCoy, Benjamin,   Kentucky   Barren County
        McCoy, Benjamin,   over 21 Male
        Color: White
Acres of land: 200; Barren Co.; watercourse: Mill Creek; Entry: Benjm McCoy; Survey: same; Patent: 0; white males over 21: 1; white males 16-21: 0; blacks over 16: 0; total blacks: 0; horses: 1; stud horses: 0; retail stores: 0; tavern license: 0.
Barren County Tax Book, 1800, part 1 - page: 10
FAMILY HISTORY LIBRARY film 7865
McEntire,   Kentucky   Barren County?
        McEntire,   Male
The entry for land owned by John How was in his name.
Barren County Tax Book, 1800, part 1 - page: 7
FAMILY HISTORY LIBRARY film 7865

McFerren, John, Kentucky Barren County

McFerren, John, over 21 Male **Color:** White

slave, over 16 Male **Color:** Colored

Acres: 0; County: 0; watercourse: 0; Entry: 0; Survey: 0; Patent: 0; white males over 21: 1; white males 16-21: 0; blacks over 16: 1; total blacks: 1; horses: 5; stud horses: 0; retail store: 0; tavern lic.: 0.

Barren County Tax Book, 1800, part 1 - page: 11
FAMILY HISTORY LIBRARY film 7865

McGee, Henry, Kentucky Barren County

McGee, Henry, over 21 Male **Color:** White

Acres of land: 0; County: 0; watercourse: 0; Entry: 0; Survey: 0; Patent: 0; white males over 21: 1; white males 16-21: 0; blacks over 16: 0; total blacks: 0; horses: 3; stud horses: 0; retail stores: 0; tavern license: 0.

Barren County Tax Book, 1800, part 1 - page: 10
FAMILY HISTORY LIBRARY film 7865

McGee, John, Kentucky Barren County

McGee, John, over 21 Male **Color:** White

Acres of land: 0; County: 0; watercourse: 0; Entry: 0; Survey: 0; Patent: 0; white males over 21: 1; white males 16-21: 0; blacks over 16: 0; total blacks: 0; horses: 3; stud horses: 0; retail stores: 0; tavern license: 0.

Barren County Tax Book, 1800, part 1 - page: 10
FAMILY HISTORY LIBRARY film 7865

McKenny, Josiah, Kentucky Barren County?

McKenny, Josiah, Male

The entry for land owned by John Boyd was in his name.

Barren County Tax Book, 1800, part 1 - page: 3
FAMILY HISTORY LIBRARY film 7865

McMahan, Hugh, Kentucky Barren County

McMahan, Hugh, over 21 Male **Color:** White

Acres of land: 200; Barren Co.; watercourse: Skeggs Creek; Entry: Hugh McMahan; Survey: same; Patent: 0; white males over 21: 1; white males 16-21: 0; blacks over 16: 0; total blacks: 0; horses: 3; stud horses: 0; retail stores: 0; tavern license: 0.

Barren County Tax Book, 1800, part 1 - page: 10
FAMILY HISTORY LIBRARY film 7865

McMahan, Martin, Kentucky Barren County

McMahan, Martin, 16-21 Male **Color:** White

Acres: 0; County: 0; watercourse: 0; Entry: 0; Survey: 0; Patent: 0; white males over 21: 0; white males 16-21: 1; blacks over 16: 0; total blacks: 0; horses: 1; stud horses: 0; retail store: 0; tavern lic.: 0.

Barren County Tax Book, 1800, part 1 - page: 11
FAMILY HISTORY LIBRARY film 7865

McManus, Patrick, Kentucky Barren County

McManus, Patrick, over 21 Male **Color:** White

Acres of land: 200; Barren Co.; watercourse: Fallen Timber; Entry: Patrick McManus; Survey: same; Patent: 0; white males over 21: 1; white males 16-21: 0; blacks over 16: 0; total blacks: 0; horses: 6; stud horses: 0; retail stores: 0; tavern license: 0.

Barren County Tax Book, 1800, part 1 - page: 10
FAMILY HISTORY LIBRARY film 7865

McMurry, Mary, Kentucky Barren County

McMurry, Mary, Female

Acres of land: 0; County: 0; watercourse: 0; Entry: 0; Survey: 0; Patent: 0; white males over 21: 0; white males 16-21: 0; blacks over 16: 0; total blacks: 0; horses: 3; stud horses: 0; retail stores: 0; tavern license: 0.

Barren County Tax Book, 1800, part 1 - page: 10
FAMILY HISTORY LIBRARY film 7865

McQueen, Benjamin, Kentucky Barren County

McQueen, Benjamin, over 21 Male **Color:** White

Acres of land: 200; Barren Co.; watercourse: 0; Entry: Benjamin McQueen; Survey: 0; Patent: 0; white males over 21: 1; white males 16-21: 0; blacks over 16: 0; total blacks: 0; horses: 1; stud horses: 0; retail stores: 0; tavern license: 0.

Barren County Tax Book, 1800, part 1 - page: 10
FAMILY HISTORY LIBRARY film 7865

Means, Isaac, Kentucky Barren County

Means, Isaac, over 21 Male **Color:** White

Acres of land: 100; Barren Co.; watercourse: Mill Creek; Entry: Isaac Means; Survey: same; Patent: 0; white males over 21: 1; white males 16-21: 0; blacks over 16: 0; total blacks: 0; horses: 2; stud horses: 0; retail stores: 0; tavern license: 0.
Barren County Tax Book, 1800, part 1 - page: 10
FAMILY HISTORY LIBRARY film 7865
Means, Thomas, Kentucky Barren County
 Means, Thomas, over 21 Male
 Color: White
Acres of land: 200; Barren Co.; watercourse: E F Mill Creek; Entry: Thos Means; Survey: same; Patent: 0; white males over 21: 1; white males 16-21: 0; blacks over 16: 0; total blacks: 0; horses: 2; stud horses: 0; retail stores: 0; tavern license: 0.
Barren County Tax Book, 1800, part 1 - page: 10
FAMILY HISTORY LIBRARY film 7865
Mercer, Forester, Kentucky Barren County
 Mercer, Forester, over 21 Male
 Color: White
Acres of land: 0; Barren Co.; watercourse: 0; Entry: 0; Survey: 0; Patent: 0; white males over 21: 1; white males 16-21: 0; blacks over 16: 0; total blacks: 0; horses: 2; stud horses: 0; retail stores: 0; tavern license: 0.
Barren County Tax Book, 1800, part 1 - page: 10
FAMILY HISTORY LIBRARY film 7865
Mercer, Howard, Kentucky Barren County
 Mercer, Howard, over 21 Male
 Color: White
Acres of land: 100; Barren Co.; watercourse: Mill Creek; Entry: Howard Mercer; Survey: same; Patent: 0; white males over 21: 1; white males 16-21: 0; blacks over 16: 0; total blacks: 0; horses: 1; stud horses: 0; retail stores: 0; tavern license: 0.
Barren County Tax Book, 1800, part 1 - page: 10
FAMILY HISTORY LIBRARY film 7865
Mershon, Andrew, Kentucky Barren County
 Mershon, Andrew, over 21 Male
 Color: White
Acres of land: 0; County: 0; watercourse: 0; Entry: 0; Survey: 0; Patent: 0; white males over 21: 1; white males 16-21: 0; blacks over 16: 0; total blacks: 0; horses: 1; stud horses: 0; retail stores: 0; tavern license: 0.

Barren County Tax Book, 1800, part 1 - page: 10
FAMILY HISTORY LIBRARY film 7865
Mershon, Benjamin, Kentucky Barren County
 Mershon, Benjamin, over 21 Male
 Color: White
Acres of land: 142 1/2; Barren Co.; watercourse: 0; Entry: Jas Crawford; Survey: same; Patent: same; white males over 21: 1; white males 16-21: 0; blacks over 16: 0; total blacks: 0; horses: 6; stud horses: 0; retail stores: 0; tavern license: 0.
Barren County Tax Book, 1800, part 1 - page: 10
FAMILY HISTORY LIBRARY film 7865
Mershon, Timothy, Kentucky Barren County
 Mershon, Timothy, over 21 Male
 Color: White
Acres of land: 0; County: 0; watercourse: 0; Entry: 0; Survey: 0; Patent: 0; white males over 21: 1; white males 16-21: 0; blacks over 16: 0; total blacks: 0; horses: 0; stud horses: 0; retail stores: 0; tavern license: 0.
Barren County Tax Book, 1800, part 1 - page: 10
FAMILY HISTORY LIBRARY film 7865
Middleton, John, Kentucky Barren County
 Middleton, John, over 21 Male
 Color: White
 Middleton, over 21 Male **Color:** White
 Middleton, 16-21 Male **Color:** White
 slave, over 16 Male **Color:** Colored
Acres: 200; County: Barren; watercourse: Peters Creek; Entry: Thos Middleton; Survey: same; Patent: 0; white males over 21: 2; white males 16-21: 1; blacks over 16: 1; total blacks: 3; horses: 5; stud horses: 0; retail store: 0; tavern lic.: 0.
Barren County Tax Book, 1800, part 1 - page: 11
FAMILY HISTORY LIBRARY film 7865
Middleton, Thos, Kentucky Barren County?
 Middleton, Thos, Male
The entry for land owned by John Middleton was in his name.
Barren County Tax Book, 1800, part 1 - page: 11
FAMILY HISTORY LIBRARY film 7865
Minor, Thomas, Kentucky Barren County?
 Minor, Thomas, Male

The entry for land owned by James Crawford was in his name.

Barren County Tax Book, 1800, part 1 - page: 4
FAMILY HISTORY LIBRARY film 7865
Mitchel, Moses,   Kentucky   Barren County

     Mitchel, Moses,   over 21 Male
     Color: White
     Mitchel,   16-21 Male **Color:** White
     Mitchel,   16-21 Male **Color:** White
     slave, over 16 Male **Color:** Colored

Acres: 200; County: Barren; watercourse: E F Big Barren; Entry: Nathan Wood; Survey: same; Patent: 0; white males over 21: 1; white males 16-21: 2; blacks over 16: 1; total blacks: 1; horses: 4; stud horses: 0; retail store: 0; tavern lic.: 0.
Barren County Tax Book, 1800, part 1 - page: 11
FAMILY HISTORY LIBRARY film 7865
Mitchel, Moses,   Kentucky   Barren County

     Mitchel, Moses,   Male

Acres: 150; County: Barren; watercourse: Big Bone Lick; Entry: Jas Grimes; Survey: Jas Grimes; Patent: J. Mathews & M. Mitchel; white males over 21: 0; white males 16-21: 0; blacks over 16: 0; total blacks: 0; horses: 0; stud horses: 0; tavern: 0.
Barren County Tax Book, 1800, part 1 - page: 11
FAMILY HISTORY LIBRARY film 7865
Mitchel, William,   Kentucky   Barren County

     Mitchel, William,   over 21 Male
     Color: White

Acres of land: 200; Barren Co.; watercourse: Mill Creek; Entry: Wm Mitchel; Survey: same; Patent: 0; white males over 21: 1; white males 16-21: 0; blacks over 16: 0; total blacks: 1; horses: 2; stud horses: 0; retail stores: 0; tavern license: 0.
Barren County Tax Book, 1800, part 1 - page: 10
FAMILY HISTORY LIBRARY film 7865
Morris, James,   Kentucky   Barren County

     Morris, James, over 21 Male **Color:** White

Acres of land: 200; Barren Co.; watercourse: E F Big Barren; Entry: Jas Morris; Survey: same; Patent: 0; white males over 21: 1; white males 16-

21: 0; blacks over 16: 0; total blacks: 0; horses: 3; stud horses: 0; retail stores: 0; tavern license: 0.
Barren County Tax Book, 1800, part 1 - page: 10
FAMILY HISTORY LIBRARY film 7865
Morris, Richard,   Kentucky   Barren County

     Morris, Richard,   over 21 Male
     Color: White

Acres: 200; County: Barren; watercourse: Peters Creek; Entry: Richd Morris; Survey: same; Patent: 0; white males over 21: 1; white males 16-21: 0; blacks over 16: 0; total blacks: 0; horses: 1; stud horses: 0; retail store: 0; tavern lic.: 0.
Barren County Tax Book, 1800, part 1 - page: 11
FAMILY HISTORY LIBRARY film 7865
Moss, Ted?,   Kentucky   Barren County

     Moss, Ted?,   over 21 Male **Color:** White
     slave, over 16 Male **Color:** Colored

Acres of land: 200; Barren Co.; watercourse: S. F. Bear? Creek; Entry: John Scott; Survey: same; Patents: same; white males over 21: 1; white males 16-21: 0; blacks over 16: 1; total blacks: 2; horses: 5; stud horses: 0; retail stores: 0; tavern lic.: 0.
Barren County Tax Book, 1800, part 1 - page: 11
FAMILY HISTORY LIBRARY film 7865
Mulkey, John, Kentucky   Barren County

     Mulkey, John, over 21 Male **Color:** White

Acres of land: 200; Barren Co.; watercourse: Mill Creek; Entry: Jno Mulkey; Survey: same; Patent: 0; white males over 21: 1; white males 16-21: 0; blacks over 16: 0; total blacks: 0; horses: 2; stud horses: 0; retail stores: 0; tavern license: 0.
Barren County Tax Book, 1800, part 1 - page: 10
FAMILY HISTORY LIBRARY film 7865
Mulkey, Philip,   Kentucky   Barren County

     Mulkey, Philip, over 21 Male **Color:** White

Acres of land: 100; Barren Co.; watercourse: Mill Creek; Entry: Philip Mulkey; Survey: same; Patent: 0; white males over 21: 1; white males 16-21: 0; blacks over 16: 0; total blacks: 0; horses: 3; stud horses: 0; retail stores: 0; tavern license: 0.
Barren County Tax Book, 1800, part 1 - page: 10
FAMILY HISTORY LIBRARY film 7865
Musick, Thomas,   Kentucky   Barren County

Musick, Thomas,   over 21 Male
Color: White
Acres of land: 100; Barren Co.; watercourse: Bluespring Creek; Entry: Thos Musick; Survey: 0; Patent: 0; white males over 21: 1; white males 16-21: 0; blacks over 16: 0; total blacks: 0; horses: 3; stud horses: 0; retail stores: 0; tavern license: 0.
Barren County Tax Book, 1800, part 1 - page: 10
FAMILY HISTORY LIBRARY film 7865
Neal, Thos,   Kentucky   Barren County?
        Neal, Thos,   Male
The entry for land owned by Thomas Fliping was in his name.
Barren County Tax Book, 1800, part 1 - page: 6
FAMILY HISTORY LIBRARY film 7865
Nelson, Joel,   Kentucky   Barren County
        Nelson, Joel,   over 21 Male   **Color:** White
Acres: 0; County: 0; watercourse: 0; Entry: 0; Survey: 0; Patent: 0; white males over 21: 1; white males 16-21: 0; blacks over 16: 0; total blacks: 0; horses: 1; stud horses: 0; retail store: 0; tavern lic.: 0.
Barren County Tax Book, 1800, part 1 - page: 11
FAMILY HISTORY LIBRARY film 7865
Nelson, John, Kentucky   Barren County
        Nelson, John,   over 21 Male   **Color:** White
Acres: 0; County: 0; watercourse: 0; Entry: 0; Survey: 0; Patent: 0; white males over 21: 1; white males 16-21: 0; blacks over 16: 0; total blacks: 0; horses: 1; stud horses: 0; retail store: 0; tavern lic.: 0.
Barren County Tax Book, 1800, part 1 - page: 11
FAMILY HISTORY LIBRARY film 7865
Nevil, James, Kentucky   Barren County
        Nevil, James,   Male
Acres: 500; County: 0; watercourse: Licking; Entry: 0; Survey: 0; Patent: 0; white males over 21: 0; white males 16-21: 0; blacks over 16: 0; total blacks: 0; horses: 0; stud horses: 0; retail store: 0; tavern lic.: 0.
Barren County Tax Book, 1800, part 1 - page: 11
FAMILY HISTORY LIBRARY film 7865
Nevil, James, Kentucky   Barren County
        Nevil, James,   over 21 Male   **Color:** White
        Nevil,   16-21   Male   **Color:** White
Acres: 200; County: Barren;   watercourse: Bluespring Creek; Entry: Jas Nevil; Survey: same;

Patent: 0; white males over 21: 1; white males 16-21: 1; blacks over 16: 0; total blacks: 0; horses: 3; stud horses: 0; retail store: 0; tavern lic.: 0.
Barren County Tax Book, 1800, part 1 - page: 11
FAMILY HISTORY LIBRARY film 7865
Nevil, James, Kentucky   Barren County
        Nevil, James,   Male
Acres: 666 2/3; County: 0; watercourse: Lick Creek; Entry: Jas Nevil; Survey: same; Patent: 0; white males over 21: 0; white males 16-21: 0; blacks over 16: 0; total blacks: 0; horses: 0; stud horses: 0; retail store: 0; tavern lic.: 0.
Barren County Tax Book, 1800, part 1 - page: 11
FAMILY HISTORY LIBRARY film 7865
Nevil, Jas,   Kentucky   Barren County?
        Nevil, Jas,   Male
The entry for land owned by Dudley Roundtree senr was in his name.
Barren County Tax Book, 1800, part 1 - page: 12
FAMILY HISTORY LIBRARY film 7865
Nevil, William,   Kentucky   Barren County
        Nevil, William, over 21 Male   **Color:** White
        slave,   over 16 Male   **Color:** Colored
        slave,   over 16 Male   **Color:** Colored
Acres: 200; County: Barren; watercourse: Beaver Creek; Entry: Wm Nevil; Survey: same; Patent: 0; white males over 21: 1; white males 16-21: 0; blacks over 16: 2; total blacks: 3; horses: 3; stud horses: 0; retail store: 0; tavern lic.: 0.
Barren County Tax Book, 1800, part 1 - page: 11
FAMILY HISTORY LIBRARY film 7865
Newell, Samuel,   Kentucky   Barren County?
        Newell, Samuel,   Male
On 16 Jun 1792 he was made a Justice of the Peace for Knox County (in Tennessee).
"An early settler, from Virginia, in the Holston Valley; an active officer in the border warfare of the Revolution; one of the founders of and an officer in the State of Franklin; a member of the first Tennessee Assembly; removed to Kentucky, 1797 (Williams, [Lost State of Franklin,] pp. 315-316)."
Territorial Papers of the US - volume: 4 page: 449
Nobblit, Isaac, Kentucky   Barren County
        Nobblit, Isaac,   over 21 Male   **Color:** White

Acres: 0; County: 0; watercourse: 0; Entry: 0; Survey: 0; Patent: 0; white males over 21: 1; white males 16-21: 0; blacks over 16: 0; total blacks: 0; horses: 1; stud horses: 0; retail store: 0; tavern lic.: 0.
Barren County Tax Book, 1800, part 1 - page: 11
FAMILY HISTORY LIBRARY film 7865
Norvil?, Lipscom,   Kentucky   Barren County?
      Norvil?, Lipscom,   Male
The entry for land owned by Leonard Hall was in his name.
Barren County Tax Book, 1800, part 1 - page: 7
FAMILY HISTORY LIBRARY film 7865
Osborn, Solamon,   Kentucky   Barren County
      Osborn, Solamon,   over 21 Male
      Color: White
Acres: 0; County: 0; watercourse: 0; Entry: 0; Survey: 0; Patent: 0; white males over 21: 1; white males 16-21: 0; blacks over 16: 0; total blacks: 0; horses: 1; stud horses: 0; retail store: 0; tavern lic.: 0.
Barren County Tax Book, 1800, part 1 - page: 11
FAMILY HISTORY LIBRARY film 7865
Pale?, Peter,   Kentucky   Barren County
      Pale?, Peter,   over 21 Male   **Color:** White
Acres of land: 0; Barren Co.; watercourse: 0; Entry: 0; Survey: 0; Patents: 0; white males over 21: 1; white males 16-21: 0; blacks over 16: 0; total blacks: 0; horses: 1; stud horses: 0; retail stores: 0; tavern license: 0.
Barren County Tax Book, 1800, part 1 - page: 1
FAMILY HISTORY LIBRARY film 7865
Parke, Samuel,   Kentucky   Barren County
      Parke, Samuel, over 21 Male   **Color:** White
Acres: 150; County: Barrren; watercourse: Little Barren; Entry: Saml Parke; Survey: same; Patent: 0; white males over 21: 1; white males 16-21: 0; blacks over 16: 0; total blacks: 0; horses: 2; stud horses: 0; retail store: 0; tavern lic.: 0.
Barren County Tax Book, 1800, part 1 - page: 11
FAMILY HISTORY LIBRARY film 7865
Parsons, Thomas,   Kentucky   Barren County
      Parsons, Thomas,   over 21 Male
      Color: White

Acres: 0; County: 0; watercourse: 0; Entry: 0; Survey: 0; Patent: 0; white males over 21: 1; white males 16-21: 0; blacks over 16: 0; total blacks: 0; horses: 1; stud horses: 0; retail store: 0; tavern lic.: 0.
Barren County Tax Book, 1800, part 1 - page: 11
FAMILY HISTORY LIBRARY film 7865
Payn, Sylvester,   Kentucky   Barren County?
      Payn, Sylvester,   Male
The entry for land owned by Daniel Curd was in his name.
Barren County Tax Book, 1800, part 1 - page: 3
FAMILY HISTORY LIBRARY film 7865
Pennington, Joshua,   Kentucky   Barren County
      Pennington, Joshua,   over 21 Male
      Color: White
Acres: 0; County: 0; watercourse: 0; Entry: 0; Survey: 0; Patent: 0; white males over 21: 1; white males 16-21: 0; blacks over 16: 0; total blacks: 0; horses: 1; stud horses: 0; retail store: 0; tavern lic.: 0.
Barren County Tax Book, 1800, part 1 - page: 11
FAMILY HISTORY LIBRARY film 7865
Pennington, Richard,   Kentucky   Barren County
      Pennington, Richard,   over 21 Male
      Color: White
      Pennington,   16-21   Male   **Color:** White
Acres: 0; County: 0; watercourse: 0; Entry: 0; Survey: 0; Patent: 0; white males over 21: 1; white males 16-21: 1; blacks over 16: 0; total blacks: 0; horses: 2; stud horses: 0; retail store: 0; tavern lic.: 0.
Barren County Tax Book, 1800, part 1 - page: 11
FAMILY HISTORY LIBRARY film 7865
Perkins, Ann,   Kentucky   Barren County?
      Perkins, Ann,   Female
The entry for land owned by William Perkins was in her name.
Barren County Tax Book, 1800, part 1 - page: 11
FAMILY HISTORY LIBRARY film 7865
Perkins, Jesse, Kentucky   Barren County
      Perkins, Jesse,   Male
The entry for land owned by William Perkins was in his name.
Barren County Tax Book, 1800, part 1 - page: 11
FAMILY HISTORY LIBRARY film 7865

Perkins, William, Kentucky Barren County

      Perkins, William, Male

Acres: 200; County: Barrren; watercourse: Skeggs Creek; Entry: Wm Perkins; Survey: same; Patent: 0; white males over 21: 0; white males 16-21: 0; blacks over 16: 0; total blacks: 0; horses: 0; stud horses: 0; retail store: 0; tavern lic.: 0.

Barren County Tax Book, 1800, part 1 - page: 11
FAMILY HISTORY LIBRARY film 7865

Perkins, William, Kentucky Barren County

      Perkins, William, Male

Acres: 150; County: Barren; watercourse: Fallen Timber; Entry: Jesse Perkins; Survey: same; Patent: 0; white males over 21: 0; white males 16-21: 0; blacks over 16: 0; total blacks: 0; horses: 0; stud horses: 0; retail store: 0; tavern lic.: 0.

Barren County Tax Book, 1800, part 1 - page: 11
FAMILY HISTORY LIBRARY film 7865

Perkins, William, Kentucky Barren County

      Perkins, William, over 21 Male **Color:** White

      Perkins, 16-21 Male **Color:** White

     slave, over 16 Male **Color:** Colored

     slave, over 16 Male **Color:** Colored

Acres: 200; County: Barren; watercourse: Fallen Timber; Entry: Ann Perkins; Survey: Wm Perkins; Patent: 0; white males over 21: 1; white males 16-21: 1; blacks over 16: 2; total blacks: 5; horses: 7; stud horses: 0; retail store: 0; tavern lic.: 0.

Barren County Tax Book, 1800, part 1 - page: 11
FAMILY HISTORY LIBRARY film 7865

Perkins, Wm, Kentucky Barren County

      Perkins, Wm, Male

The entry for land owned by Joseph Martin was in his name.

Barren County Tax Book, 1800, part 1 - page: 11
FAMILY HISTORY LIBRARY film 7865

Perry, James, Kentucky Barren County

      Perry, James, Male

Acres: 100; County: Barren; watercourse: 0; Entry: Jas Perry; Survey: same; Patent: 0; white males over 21: 0; white males 16-21: 0; blacks over 16: 0; total blacks: 0; horses: 0; stud horses: 0; retail store: 0; tavern lic.: 0.

Barren County Tax Book, 1800, part 1 - page: 12
FAMILY HISTORY LIBRARY film 7865

Perry, James, Kentucky Barren County

      Perry, James, over 21 Male **Color:** White

Acres: 200; County: Barren; watercourse: 0; Entry: Jas Perry; Survey: same; Patent: 0; white males over 21: 1; white males 16-21: 0; blacks over 16: 0; total blacks: 0; horses: 1; stud horses: 0; retail store: 0; tavern lic.: 0.

Barren County Tax Book, 1800, part 1 - page: 12
FAMILY HISTORY LIBRARY film 7865

Pinkley, John, Kentucky Barren County

      Pinkley, John, over 21 Male **Color:** White

Acres: 0; County: 0; watercourse: 0; Entry: 0; Survey: 0; Patent: 0; white males over 21: 1; white males 16-21: 0; blacks over 16: 0; total blacks: 0; horses: 1; stud horses: 0; retail store: 0; tavern lic.: 0.

Barren County Tax Book, 1800, part 1 - page: 11
FAMILY HISTORY LIBRARY film 7865

Ponor, Gabriel, Kentucky Barren County?

      Ponor, Gabriel, Male

The entry for land owned by Edmond Rogers was in his name.

Barren County Tax Book, 1800, part 1 - page: 13
FAMILY HISTORY LIBRARY film 7865

Ponor, Geo, Kentucky Barren County?

      Ponor, Geo, Male

The entry for land owned by Edmond Rogers was in his name.

Barren County Tax Book, 1800, part 1 - page: 13
FAMILY HISTORY LIBRARY film 7865

Ponor?, Jos, Kentucky Barren County?

      Ponor?, Jos, Male

The patent for land owned by Edmond Rogers was in his name.

Barren County Tax Book, 1800, part 1 - page: 13
FAMILY HISTORY LIBRARY film 7865

Proctor, William, Kentucky Barren County

      Proctor, William, over 21 Male **Color:** White

Acres: 200; County: Barren; watercourse: E F Big Barren; Entry: Wm Proctor; Survey: same; Patent: 0; white males over 21: 1; white males 16-21: 0; blacks over 16: 0; total blacks: 0; horses: 3; stud horses: 0; retail store: 0; tavern lic.: 0.

Barren County Tax Book, 1800, part 1 - page: 12
FAMILY HISTORY LIBRARY film 7865

Pryor, John, Kentucky Barren County?
Pryor, John, Male
The entry and survey for land owned by Edmond Rogers was in his name.
Barren County Tax Book, 1800, part 1 - page: 13
FAMILY HISTORY LIBRARY film 7865

Radford, Elijah, Kentucky Barren County
Radford, Elijah, over 21 Male
Color: White
Acres: 200; County: Barren; watercourse: No Bob; Entry: E Radford; Survey: same; Patent: 0; white males over 21: 1; white males 16-21: 0; blacks over 16: 0; total blacks: 0; horses: 3; stud horses: 0; retail store: 0; tavern lic.: 0.
Barren County Tax Book, 1800, part 1 - page: 13
FAMILY HISTORY LIBRARY film 7865

Railsback, John, Kentucky Barren County
Railsback, John, over 21 Male
Color: White
Railsback, 16-21 Male **Color:** White
Acres: 200; County: Barren; watercourse: Marrowbone; Entry: John Railsback; Survey: same; Patent: 0; white males over 21: 1; white males 16-21: 1; blacks over 16: 0; total blacks: 0; horses: 3; stud horses: 0; retail store: 0; tavern lic.: 0.
Barren County Tax Book, 1800, part 1 - page: 13
FAMILY HISTORY LIBRARY film 7865

Raimsy, John, Kentucky Barren County
Raimsy, John, over 21 Male **Color:** White
Acres: 0; County: 0; watercourse: 0; Entry: 0; Survey: 0; Patent: 0; white males over 21: 1; white males 16-21: 0; blacks over 16: 0; total blacks: 0; horses: 1; stud horses: 0; retail store: 0; tavern lic.: 0.
Barren County Tax Book, 1800, part 1 - page: 12
FAMILY HISTORY LIBRARY film 7865

Rasdal, William, Senr Kentucky Barren County
Rasdal, William, Senr over 21 Male
Color: White
Acres: 0; County: 0; watercourse: 0; Entry: 0; Survey: 0; Patent: 0; white males over 21: 1; white males 16-21: 0; blacks over 16: 0; total blacks: 0; horses: 2; stud horses: 0; retail store: 0; tavern lic.: 0.

Barren County Tax Book, 1800, part 1 - page: 12
FAMILY HISTORY LIBRARY film 7865

Ratcliffe, William, Kentucky Barren County
Ratcliffe, William, over 21 Male
Color: White
Acres: 200; County: Barren; watercourse: 0; Entry: Wm Ratcliffe; Survey: same; Patent: 0; white males over 21: 1; white males 16-21: 0; blacks over 16: 0; total blacks: 0; horses: 2; stud horses: 0; retail store: 0; tavern lic.: 0.
Barren County Tax Book, 1800, part 1 - page: 12
FAMILY HISTORY LIBRARY film 7865

Renick, Henry, Kentucky Barren County
Renick, Henry, Male
Acres: 166; County: Barren; watercourse: Bluespring Creek; Entry: Henry Renick; Survey: same; Patent: same; white males over 21: 0; white males 16-21: 0; blacks over 16: 0; total blacks: 0; horses: 0; stud horses: 0; retail store: 0; tavern: 0.
Barren County Tax Book, 1800, part 1 - page: 12
FAMILY HISTORY LIBRARY film 7865

Renick, Henry, Kentucky Barren County
Renick, Henry, Male
Acres: 184; County: Barren; watercourse: Bluespring Creek; Entry: Abrm Chaplin; Survey: same; Patent: same; white males over 21: 0; white males 16-21: 0; blacks over 16: 0; total blacks: 0; horses: 0; stud horses: 0; retail store: 0; tavern: 0.
Barren County Tax Book, 1800, part 1 - page: 12
FAMILY HISTORY LIBRARY film 7865

Renick, Henry, Kentucky Barren County
Renick, Henry, Male
Acres: 200; County: Barren; watercourse: Russells Creek; Entry: Saml Tipton; Survey: same; Patent: Henry Renick; white males over 21: 0; white males 16-21: 0; blacks over 16: 0; total blacks: 0; horses: 0; stud horses: 0; retail store: 0; tavern lic.: 0.
Barren County Tax Book, 1800, part 1 - page: 12
FAMILY HISTORY LIBRARY film 7865

Renick, Henry, Kentucky Barren County
Renick, Henry, Male
Acres: 374; County: Cumberland; watercourse: Renicks Creek; Entry: Saml Tipton; Survey: same; Patent: Henry Renick; white males over 21: 0; white males 16-21: 0; blacks over 16: 0; total

blacks: 0; horses: 0; stud horses: 0; retail store: 0; tavern: 0.
Barren County Tax Book, 1800, part 1 - page: 12
FAMILY HISTORY LIBRARY film 7865
Renick, Henry, Kentucky Barren County
     Renick, Henry, Male
Acres: 121 1/3; County: Green; watercourse: Russells Creek; Entry: Henry Rinick; Survey: same; Patent: same; white males over 21: 0; white males 16-21: 0; blacks over 16: 0; total blacks: 0; horses: 0; stud horses: 0; retail store: 0; tavern lic.: 0.
Barren County Tax Book, 1800, part 1 - page: 12
FAMILY HISTORY LIBRARY film 7865
Renick, Henry, Kentucky Barren County?
     Renick, Henry, Male
The entry for land owned by Joseph Jones was in his name.
Barren County Tax Book, 1800, part 1 - page: 8
FAMILY HISTORY LIBRARY film 7865
Renick, Henry, Kentucky Barren County
     Renick, Henry, over 21 Male **Color:** White
     slave, over 16 Male **Color:** Colored
     slave, over 16 Male **Color:** Colored
Acres: 400; County: Green; watercourse: Russells Creek; Entry: Saml Tipton; Survey: same; Patent: same; white males over 21: 1; white males 16-21: 0; blacks over 16: 2; total blacks: 5; horses: 9; stud horses: 0; retail store: 0; tavern lic.: 0.
Barren County Tax Book, 1800, part 1 - page: 12
FAMILY HISTORY LIBRARY film 7865
Renick, James, Kentucky Barren County
     Renick, James, over 21 Male **Color:** White
     Renick, over 21 Male **Color:** White
Acres: 200; County: Barren; watercourse: Swearingans fork; Entry: Jas Renick; Survey: same; Patent: 0; white males over 21: 2; white males 16-21: 0; blacks over 16: 0; total blacks: 0; horses: 4; stud horses: 0; retail store: 0; tavern lic.: 0.
Barren County Tax Book, 1800, part 1 - page: 12
FAMILY HISTORY LIBRARY film 7865
Renick, Saml, Kentucky Barren County?

     Renick, Saml, Male
The entry for land owned by William Renick was in his name.
Barren County Tax Book, 1800, part 1 - page: 12
FAMILY HISTORY LIBRARY film 7865
Renick, Samuel, senr Kentucky Barren County
     Renick, Samuel, senr Male
Acres: 100; County: Mercer; watercourse: Doctors fork; Entry: 0; Survey: 0; Patent: 0; white males over 21: 0; white males 16-21: 0; blacks over 16: 0; total blacks: 0; horses: 0; stud horses: 0; retail store: 0; tavern lic.: 0.
Barren County Tax Book, 1800, part 1 - page: 13
FAMILY HISTORY LIBRARY film 7865
Renick, Samuel, senr Kentucky Barren County
     Renick, Samuel, senr over 21 Male **Color:** White
     slave, over 16 Male **Color:** Colored
Acres: 200; County: Barren; watercourse: 0; Entry: David Warren; Survey: same; Patent: same; white males over 21: 1; white males 16-21: 0; blacks over 16: 1; total blacks: 1; horses: 4; stud horses: 0; retail store: 0; tavern lic.: 0.
Barren County Tax Book, 1800, part 1 - page: 13
FAMILY HISTORY LIBRARY film 7865
Renick, Samuel, senr Kentucky Barren County
     Renick, Samuel, senr Male
Acres: 200; County: Barren; watercourse: 0; Entry: Saml Davis; Survey: same; Patent: 0; white males over 21: 0; white males 16-21: 0; blacks over 16: 0; total blacks: 0; horses: 0; stud horses: 0; retail store: 0; tavern lic.: 0.
Barren County Tax Book, 1800, part 1 - page: 13
FAMILY HISTORY LIBRARY film 7865
Renick, Samuel, senr Kentucky Barren County
     Renick, Samuel, senr Male
Acres: 100; County: Warren; watercourse: 0; Entry: 0; Survey: 0; Patent: 0; white males over 21: 0; white males 16-21: 0; blacks over 16: 0; total blacks: 0; horses: 0; stud horses: 0; retail store: 0; tavern lic.: 0.
Barren County Tax Book, 1800, part 1 - page: 13
FAMILY HISTORY LIBRARY film 7865
Renick, Thomas, Kentucky Barren County

Renick, Thomas,   over 21 Male
Color: White
Acres: 200; County: Barren; watercourse: Fallen Timber; Entry: Thos Renick; Survey: same; Patent: 0; white males over 21: 1; white males 16-21: 0; blacks over 16: 0; total blacks: 0; horses: 4; stud horses: 0; retail store: 0; tavern lic.: 0.
Barren County Tax Book, 1800, part 1 - page: 12
FAMILY HISTORY LIBRARY film 7865
Renick, William,   Kentucky   Barren County
    Renick, William,   Male
Acres: 92; County: Barren; watercourse: Bluespring Creek; Entry: Abrhm Chaplin; Survey: same; Patent: same; white males over 21: 0; white males 16-21: 0; blacks over 16: 0; total blacks: 0; horses: 0; stud horses: 0; retail store: 0; tavern: 0.
Barren County Tax Book, 1800, part 1 - page: 12
FAMILY HISTORY LIBRARY film 7865
Renick, William,   Kentucky   Barren County
    Renick, William,   over 21 Male
    Color: White
    slave, over 16 Male   **Color:** Colored
Acres: 100; County: Barren; watercourse: Bluespring Creek; Entry: Saml Renick; Survey: same; Patent: same; white males over 21: 1; white males 16-21: 0; blacks over 16: 1; total blacks: 2; horses: 9; stud horses: 0; retail store: 0; tavern: 0.
Barren County Tax Book, 1800, part 1 - page: 12
FAMILY HISTORY LIBRARY film 7865
Renick?, Wm, Kentucky   Barren County?
    Renick?, Wm, Male
The entry for land owned by John Garnett was in his name.
Barren County Tax Book, 1800, part 1 - page: 6
FAMILY HISTORY LIBRARY film 7865
Rhea, Elizaberth,   Kentucky   Barren County
    Rhea, Elizaberth,   Female
    Rhea, 16-21 Male   **Color:** White
    Rhea, 16-21 Male   **Color:** White
Acres: 125; County: Barren; watercourse: 0; Entry: Eliza Rhea; Survey: same; Patent: 0; white males over 21: 0; white males 16-21: 2; blacks over 16: 0; total blacks: 0; horses: 4; stud horses: 0; retail store: 0; tavern lic.: 0.
Barren County Tax Book, 1800, part 1 - page: 13
FAMILY HISTORY LIBRARY film 7865
Rhea, Robert, Kentucky   Barren County

Rhea, Robert,   over 21 Male   **Color:** White
Acres: 0; County: 0; watercourse: 0; Entry: 0; Survey: 0; Patent: 0; white males over 21: 1; white males 16-21: 0; blacks over 16: 0; total blacks: 0; horses: 3; stud horses: 0; retail store: 0; tavern lic.: 0.
Barren County Tax Book, 1800, part 1 - page: 12
FAMILY HISTORY LIBRARY film 7865
Roberts,   Kentucky   Barren County?
    Roberts,   Male
The entry for land owned by Daniel Carter was in his name.
Barren County Tax Book, 1800, part 1 - page: 3
FAMILY HISTORY LIBRARY film 7865
Robinson, John,   Kentucky   Barren County
    Robinson, John,   Male
Acres: 200; County: Barren; watercourse: Bluespring Creek; Entry: John Robinson; Survey: same; Patent: same; white males over 21: 0; white males 16-21: 0; blacks over 16: 0; total blacks: 0; horses: 0; stud horses: 0; retail store: 0; tavern lic.: 0.
Barren County Tax Book, 1800, part 1 - page: 13
FAMILY HISTORY LIBRARY film 7865
Robinson, John,   Kentucky   Barren County
    Robinson, John,   Male
Acres: 100; County: Green; watercourse: Green River; Entry: Wm Barnett; Survey: same; Patent: same; white males over 21: 0; white males 16-21: 0; blacks over 16: 0; total blacks: 0; horses: 0; stud horses: 0; retail store: 0; tavern lic.: 0.
Barren County Tax Book, 1800, part 1 - page: 13
FAMILY HISTORY LIBRARY film 7865
Robinson, John,   Kentucky   Barren County
    Robinson, John,   over 21 Male
    Color: White
    slave, over 16 Male   **Color:** Colored
Acres: 200; County: Barren; watercourse: Bluespring Creek; Entry: Thos Marshall; Survey: same; Patent: same; white males over 21: 1; white males 16-21: 0; blacks over 16: 1; total blacks: 2; horses: 2; stud horses: 0; retail store: 0; tavern lic.: 0.
Barren County Tax Book, 1800, part 1 - page: 13
FAMILY HISTORY LIBRARY film 7865

Robinson, John, Kentucky Barren County

Robinson, John, Male

Acres: 200; County: Barren; watercourse: E F Big Barren; Entry: Wm Gill Jnr; Survey: same; Patent: 0; white males over 21: 0; white males 16-21: 0; blacks over 16: 0; total blacks: 0; horses: 0; stud horses: 0; retail store: 0; tavern lic.: 0.

Barren County Tax Book, 1800, part 1 - page: 13
FAMILY HISTORY LIBRARY film 7865

Robinson, John, Kentucky Barren County

Robinson, John, Male

Acres: 200; County: Barren; watercourse: E F Big Barren; Entry: Wm Gill Senr; Survey: same; Patent: 0; white males over 21: 0; white males 16-21: 0; blacks over 16: 0; total blacks: 0; horses: 0; stud horses: 0; retail store: 0; tavern lic.: 0.

Barren County Tax Book, 1800, part 1 - page: 13
FAMILY HISTORY LIBRARY film 7865

Robinson, Wm, Kentucky Barren County?

Robinson, Wm, Male

The entry for land owned by John Crow was in his name.

Barren County Tax Book, 1800, part 1 - page: 3
FAMILY HISTORY LIBRARY film 7865

Rogers, Edmond, Kentucky Barren County

Rogers, Edmond, Male

Acres: 2000?; County: Bullit; watercourse: 0; Entry: John Rogers; Survey: same; Patent: 0; white males over 21: 0; white males 16-21: 0; blacks over 16: 0; total blacks: 0; horses: 0; stud horses: 0; tavern: 0.

Barren County Tax Book, 1800, part 1 - page: 13
FAMILY HISTORY LIBRARY film 7865

Rogers, Edmond, Kentucky Barren County

Rogers, Edmond, Male

Acres: 200?; County: Barren; watercourse: Little Barren; Entry: Thos Wilson; Survey: same; Patent: Edmd Rogers; white males over 21: 0; white males 16-21: 0; blacks over 16: 0; total blacks: 0; horses: 0; stud horses: 0; retail store: 0; tavern lic.: 0.

Barren County Tax Book, 1800, part 1 - page: 13
FAMILY HISTORY LIBRARY film 7865

Rogers, Edmond, Kentucky Barren County

Rogers, Edmond, Male

Acres: 333 1/3; County: Warren; watercourse: Drakes Creek; Entry: Preston? Taylor; Survey: same; Patent: 0; white males over 21: 0; white males 16-21: 0; blacks over 16: 0; total blacks: 0; horses: 0; stud horses: 0; tavern: 0.

Barren County Tax Book, 1800, part 1 - page: 13
FAMILY HISTORY LIBRARY film 7865

Rogers, Edmond, Kentucky Barren County

Rogers, Edmond, Male

Acres: 765 2/3; County: Barren; watercourse: Glovers Creek; Entry: P. Ingraham; Survey: same; Patent: 0; white males over 21: 0; white males 16-21: 0; blacks over 16: 0; total blacks: 0; horses: 0; stud horses: 0; tavern: 0.

Barren County Tax Book, 1800, part 1 - page: 13
FAMILY HISTORY LIBRARY film 7865

Rogers, Edmond, Kentucky Barren County

Rogers, Edmond, Male

Acres: 225; County: Barren; watercourse: 0; Entry: E Rogers, Edm Druse?; Survey: same; Patent: same; white males over 21: 0; white males 16-21: 0; blacks over 16: 0; total blacks: 0; horses: 0; stud horses: 0; tavern: 0.

Barren County Tax Book, 1800, part 1 - page: 13
FAMILY HISTORY LIBRARY film 7865

Rogers, Edmond, Kentucky Barren County

Rogers, Edmond, Male

Acres: 666 2/3; County: Warren; watercourse: Drakes Creek; Entry: Geo & Gabriel Ponor?; Survey: same; Patent: Jos Ponor?, E Rogers; white males over 21: 0; white males 16-21: 0; blacks over 16: 0; total blacks: 0; horses: 0; stud horses: 0; tavern: 0.

Barren County Tax Book, 1800, part 1 - page: 13
FAMILY HISTORY LIBRARY film 7865

Rogers, Edmond, Kentucky Barren County?

Rogers, Edmond, Male

The entry for land owned by Robert Hill was in his name.

Barren County Tax Book, 1800, part 1 - page: 7
FAMILY HISTORY LIBRARY film 7865

Rogers, Edmond, Kentucky Barren County

Rogers, Edmond, Male

Acres: 1000; County: Barren; watercourse: Big Barren; Entry: Robt Brough; Survey: same; Patent:

E Rogers & A Chapline; white males over 21: 0; white males 16-21: 0; blacks over 16: 0; total blacks: 0; horses: 0; stud horses: 0; tavern: 0.
Barren County Tax Book, 1800, part 1 - page: 13
FAMILY HISTORY LIBRARY film 7865
Rogers, Edmond, Kentucky Barren County
Rogers, Edmond, Male
Acres: 1000; County: Barren; watercourse: Glovers Creek; Entry: P. Ingraham, A Cray . . .; Survey: same; Patent: 0; white males over 21: 0; white males 16-21: 0; blacks over 16: 0; total blacks: 0; horses: 0; stud horses: 0; tavern: 0.
Barren County Tax Book, 1800, part 1 - page: 13
FAMILY HISTORY LIBRARY film 7865
Rogers, Edmond, Kentucky Barren County
Rogers, Edmond, Male
Acres: 666 2/3; County: Barren; watercourse: Skeggs Creek; Entry: Geo Slaughter; Survey: same; Patent: Edmd Rogers; white males over 21: 0; white males 16-21: 0; blacks over 16: 0; total blacks: 0; horses: 0; stud horses: 0; tavern: 0.
Barren County Tax Book, 1800, part 1 - page: 13
FAMILY HISTORY LIBRARY film 7865
Rogers, Edmond, Kentucky Barren County
Rogers, Edmond, Male
Acres: 400?; County: Warren; watercourse: 0; Entry: Presley Thornton; Survey: same; Patent: Edmd Rogers; white males over 21: 0; white males 16-21: 0; blacks over 16: 0; total blacks: 0; horses: 0; stud horses: 0; tavern: 0.
Barren County Tax Book, 1800, part 1 - page: 13
FAMILY HISTORY LIBRARY film 7865
Rogers, Edmond, Kentucky Barren County
Rogers, Edmond, over 21 Male
Color: White
slave, over 16 Male **Color:** Colored
slave, over 16 Male **Color:** Colored
Acres: 1000; County: Barren; watercourse: Little Barren; Entry: Geo R. Clarke; Survey: same; Patent: Edmd Rogers; white males over 21: 1; white males 16-21: 0; blacks over 16: 2; total blacks: 5; horses: 7; stud horses: 0; retail store: 0; tavern lic.: 0.
Barren County Tax Book, 1800, part 1 - page: 13
FAMILY HISTORY LIBRARY film 7865

Rogers, Edmond, Kentucky Barren County?
Rogers, Edmond, Male
The entry for land owned by John Garnett was in his name.
Barren County Tax Book, 1800, part 1 - page: 6
FAMILY HISTORY LIBRARY film 7865
Rogers, Edmond, Kentucky Barren County
Rogers, Edmond, Male
Acres: 666 2/3?, County: Barren; watercourse: Fallen Timber; Entry: John Pryor; Survey: John Pryor; Patent: Edmd Rogers; white males over 21: 0; white males 15-21: 0; blacks over 16: 0; total blacks: 0; horses: 0; stud horses: 0; tavern: 0.
Barren County Tax Book, 1800, part 1 - page: 13
FAMILY HISTORY LIBRARY film 7865
Rogers, Edmond, Kentucky Barren County
Rogers, Edmond, Male
Acres: 433 1/3; County: Warren; watercourse: Drakes Creek; Entry: Robt Brough; Survey: 0; Patent: 0; white males over 21: 0; white males 16-21: 0; blacks over 16: 0; total blacks: 0; horses: 0; stud horses: 0; tavern: 0.
Barren County Tax Book, 1800, part 1 - page: 13
FAMILY HISTORY LIBRARY film 7865
Rogers, Edmond, Kentucky Barren County
Rogers, Edmond, Male
Acres: 900; County: Barren; watercourse: Little Barren; Entry: Edmd Rogers, T Wilson & C Rone?; Survey: 0; Patent: Edmd Rogers; white males over 21: 0; white males 16-21: 0; blacks over 16: 0; total blacks: 0; horses: 0; stud horses: 0; tavern: 0.
Barren County Tax Book, 1800, part 1 - page: 13
FAMILY HISTORY LIBRARY film 7865
Rogers, John, Kentucky Barren County?
Rogers, John, Male
The entry for land owned by Edmond Rogers was in his name.
Barren County Tax Book, 1800, part 1 - page: 13
FAMILY HISTORY LIBRARY film 7865
Rollins, Roderik, Kentucky Barren County
Rollins, Roderik, over 21 Male
Color: White
Acres: 200; County: Barren; watercourse: Beaver Creek; Entry: Benjamin King; Survey: same;

Patent: 0; white males over 21: 1; white males 16-21: 0; blacks over 16: 0; total blacks: 0; horses: 2; stud horses: 0; retail store: 0; tavern lic.: 0.
Barren County Tax Book, 1800, part 1 - page: 12
FAMILY HISTORY LIBRARY film 7865
Rone?, C, Kentucky Barren County?
Rone?, C, Male
The entry for land owned by Edmond Rogers was in the names of Edmd Rogers, T Wilson & C Rone?.
Barren County Tax Book, 1800, part 1 - page: 13
FAMILY HISTORY LIBRARY film 7865
Rotan, John, Kentucky Barren County
Rotan, John, over 21 Male **Color:** White
Rotan, over 21 Male **Color:** White
Acres: 200; County: Barren; watercourse: 0; Entry: John Rotan; Survey: same; Patent: same; white males over 21: 2; white males 16-21: 0; blacks over 16: 0; total blacks: 0; horses: 4; stud horses: 0; retail store: 0; tavern lic.: 0.
Barren County Tax Book, 1800, part 1 - page: 12
FAMILY HISTORY LIBRARY film 7865
Rotan, John, Kentucky Barren County?
Rotan, John, Male
The entry for land owned by John Green was in his name.
Barren County Tax Book, 1800, part 1 - page: 6
FAMILY HISTORY LIBRARY film 7865
Rotan, John, Kentucky Barren County
Rotan, John, over 21 Male **Color:** White
slave, over 16 Male **Color:** Colored
Acres: 0; County: 0; watercourse: 0; Entry: 0; Survey: 0; Patent: 0; white males over 21: 1; white males 16-21: 0; blacks over 16: 1; total blacks: 1; horses: 3; stud horses: 0; retail store: 0; tavern lic.: 0.
Barren County Tax Book, 1800, part 1 - page: 12
FAMILY HISTORY LIBRARY film 7865
Rotan, John, Kentucky Barren County
Rotan, John, Male
Acres: 100; County: Barren; watercourse: 0; Entry: John Rotan; Survey: same; Patent: same; white males over 21: 0; white males 16-21: 0; blacks over 16: 0; total blacks: 0; horses: 0; stud horses: 0; retail store: 0; tavern lic.: 0.
Barren County Tax Book, 1800, part 1 - page: 12
FAMILY HISTORY LIBRARY film 7865

Rotan, William, Kentucky Barren County
Rotan, William, over 21 Male
Color: White
slave, over 16 Male **Color:** Colored
slave, over 16 Male **Color:** Colored
Acres: 0; County: 0; watercourse: 0; Entry: 0; Survey: 0; Patent: 0; white males over 21: 1; white males 16-21: 0; blacks over 16: 2; total blacks: 4; horses: 6; stud horses: 0; retail store: 0; tavern lic.: 0.
Barren County Tax Book, 1800, part 1 - page: 12
FAMILY HISTORY LIBRARY film 7865
Rotan, Wm, Kentucky Barren County?
Rotan, Wm, Male
The entry for land owned by John Houdeshilt was in his name.
Barren County Tax Book, 1800, part 1 - page: 7
FAMILY HISTORY LIBRARY film 7865
Roundtree, Dudley, Jun Kentucky Barren County
Roundtree, Dudley, Jun over 21 Male
Color: White
Acres: 334; County: Barren; watercourse: Green River; Entry: Richard Clarke; Survey: same; Patent: same; white males over 21: 1; white males 16-21: 0; blacks over 16: 0; total blacks: 0; horses: 5; stud horses: 0; retail store: 0; tavern lic.: 0.
Barren County Tax Book, 1800, part 1 - page: 12
FAMILY HISTORY LIBRARY film 7865
Roundtree, Dudley, senr Kentucky Barren County
Roundtree, Dudley, senr over 21 Male
Color: White
slave, over 16 Male **Color:** Colored
slave, over 16 Male **Color:** Colored
slave, over 16 Male **Color:** Colored
Acres: 333 1/3; County: Barren; watercourse: Green River; Entry: Richard Clarke; Survey: same; Patent: 0; white males over 21: 1; white males 16-21: 0; blacks over 16: 3; total blacks: 5; horses: 4; stud horses: 0; retail store: 0; tavern lic.: 0.
Barren County Tax Book, 1800, part 1 - page: 12
FAMILY HISTORY LIBRARY film 7865
Roundtree, Dudley, senr Kentucky Barren County
Roundtree, Dudley, senr Male
Acres: 56; County: Garrard; watercourse: Dicks River; Entry: Jas Nevil; Survey: 0; Patent: 0; white males over 21: 0; white males 16-21: 0; blacks

over 16: 0; total blacks: 0; horses: 0; stud horses: 0; retail store: 0; tavern lic.: 0.
Barren County Tax Book, 1800, part 1 - page: 12
FAMILY HISTORY LIBRARY film 7865
Roundtree, Dudley, senr   Kentucky
        Barren County
        Roundtree, Dudley, senrMale
Acres: 200; County: Madison; watercourse: Paint? Lick; Entry: 0; Survey: 0; Patent: 0; white males over 21: 0; white males 16-21: 0; blacks over 16: 0; total blacks: 0; horses: 0; stud horses: 0; retail store: 0; tavern lic.: 0.
Barren County Tax Book, 1800, part 1 - page: 12
FAMILY HISTORY LIBRARY film 7865
Roundtree, Nathaniel, Kentucky   Barren County
        Roundtree, Nathaniel,   Male
Acres: 100?; County: Barren; watercourse: Green River; Entry: Richard Clarke; Survey: same; Patent: 0; white males over 21: 0; white males 16-21: 0; blacks over 16: 0; total blacks: 0; horses: 0; stud horses: 0; retail store: 0; tavern lic.: 0.
Barren County Tax Book, 1800, part 1 - page: 12
FAMILY HISTORY LIBRARY film 7865
Roundtree, Nathaniel, Kentucky   Barren County
        Roundtree, Nathaniel,   over 21 Male
        Color: White
        Roundtree,   over 21 Male   **Color:** White
Acres: 283?; County: Barren; watercourse: Green River; Entry: Richard Clarke; Survey: same; Patent: 0; white males over 21: 2; white males 16-21: 0; blacks over 16: 0; total blacks: 0; horses: 4; stud horses: 0; retail store: 0; tavern lic.: 0.
Barren County Tax Book, 1800, part 1 - page: 12
FAMILY HISTORY LIBRARY film 7865
Rowsy, Thomas,   Kentucky   Barren County
        Rowsy, Thomas,   over 21 Male
        Color: White
Acres: 0; County: 0; watercourse: 0; Entry: 0; Survey: 0; Patent: 0; white males over 21: 1; white males 16-21: 0; blacks over 16: 0; total blacks: 0; horses: 5; stud horses: 0; retail store: 0; tavern lic.: 0.
Barren County Tax Book, 1800, part 1 - page: 12
FAMILY HISTORY LIBRARY film 7865
Runyon, Barefoot,   Kentucky   Barren County

Runyon, Barefoot,   over 21 Male
        Color: White
Acres: 0; County: 0; watercourse: 0; Entry: 0; Survey: 0; Patent: 0; white males over 21: 1; white males 16-21: 0; blacks over 16: 0; total blacks: 0; horses: 3; stud horses: 0; retail store: 0; tavern lic.: 0.
Barren County Tax Book, 1800, part 1 - page: 13
FAMILY HISTORY LIBRARY film 7865
Runyon, Michael,   Kentucky   Barren County
        Runyon, Michael,   over 21 Male
        Color: White
Acres: 0; County: 0; watercourse: 0; Entry: 0; Survey: 0; Patent: 0; white males over 21: 1; white males 16-21: 0; blacks over 16: 0; total blacks: 0; horses: 4; stud horses: 0; retail store: 0; tavern lic.: 0.
Barren County Tax Book, 1800, part 1 - page: 13
FAMILY HISTORY LIBRARY film 7865
Runyon, William,   Kentucky   Barren County
        Runyon, William,   over 21 Male
        Color: White
Acres: 0; County: 0; watercourse: 0; Entry: 0; Survey: 0; Patent: 0; white males over 21: 1; white males 16-21: 0; blacks over 16: 0; total blacks: 0; horses: 2; stud horses: 0; retail store: 0; tavern lic.: 0.
Barren County Tax Book, 1800, part 1 - page: 13
FAMILY HISTORY LIBRARY film 7865
Rush, James, Kentucky   Barren County
        Rush, James,   over 21 Male   **Color:** White
        Rush,   16-21   Male   **Color:** White
Acres: 0; County: 0; watercourse: 0; Entry: 0; Survey: 0; Patent: 0; white males over 21: 1; white males 16-21: 1; blacks over 16: 0; total blacks: 0; horses: 2; stud horses: 0; retail store: 0; tavern lic.: 0.
Barren County Tax Book, 1800, part 1 - page: 13
FAMILY HISTORY LIBRARY film 7865
Russell, Jesse, Kentucky   Barren County?
        Russell, Jesse,   Male
The entry for land owned by Alexander Lowry was in his name.
Barren County Tax Book, 1800, part 1 - page: 9
FAMILY HISTORY LIBRARY film 7865
Scott, Kentucky   Barren County?
        Scott,   Male

The entry, survey, and patent for land owned by Abner Bourne was in his name.
Barren County Tax Book, 1800, part 1 - page: 1
FAMILY HISTORY LIBRARY film 7865
Scott, Jno,　　　Kentucky　　　Barren County?
　　　Scott, Jno,　　Male
The entry for land owned by Geddeon Mayfield was in his name.
Barren County Tax Book, 1800, part 1 - page: 10
FAMILY HISTORY LIBRARY film 7865
Scott, John,　　Kentucky　　　Barren County?
　　　Scott, John,　　Male
The entry for land owned by Ted? Moss was in his name.
Barren County Tax Book, 1800, part 1 - page: 11
FAMILY HISTORY LIBRARY film 7865
Sheppord, B,　　Kentucky　　　Barren County?
　　　Sheppord, B,　　Male
The entry for land owned by William Blakey was in his name as assee of J M Sheppord.
Barren County Tax Book, 1800, part 1 - page: 1
FAMILY HISTORY LIBRARY film 7865
Sheppord, J M,　　　Kentucky　　Barren County?
　　　Sheppord, J M, Male
The entry for land owned by William Blakey was in the name of B Sheppord as assee of J M Sheppord.
Barren County Tax Book, 1800, part 1 - page: 1
FAMILY HISTORY LIBRARY film 7865
Skeggs, Henry,　　　Kentucky　　Barren County?
　　　Skeggs, Henry, Male
The entry for land owned by Henry Cook was in his name.
Barren County Tax Book, 1800, part 1 - page: 3
FAMILY HISTORY LIBRARY film 7865
Slaughter, Geo?,　　　Kentucky　　Barren County?
　　　Slaughter, Geo?,　　　Male
The entry for land owned by Edmond Rogers was in his name.
Barren County Tax Book, 1800, part 1 - page: 13
FAMILY HISTORY LIBRARY film 7865
Smith, John,　　Kentucky　　　Barren County?
　　　Smith, John,　　Male
The entry for land owned by William Feland was in his name.
Barren County Tax Book, 1800, part 1 - page: 5
FAMILY HISTORY LIBRARY film 7865

Summers, Edwin,　　　Kentucky　　　Barren County?
　　　Summers, Edwin,　　Male
The entry for land owned by William Jenkins senr was in his name.
Barren County Tax Book, 1800, part 1 - page: 9
FAMILY HISTORY LIBRARY film 7865
Taylor, Preston?,　　Kentucky　　　Barren County?
　　　Taylor, Preston?,　　Male
The entry for land owned by Edmond Rogers was in his name.
Barren County Tax Book, 1800, part 1 - page: 13
FAMILY HISTORY LIBRARY film 7865
Thomas, James,　　Kentucky　　　Barren County?
　　　Thomas, James,　　Male
The entry for land owned by James Barten was in his name.
Barren County Tax Book, 1800, part 1 - page: 2
FAMILY HISTORY LIBRARY film 7865
Thornton, Presley,　　Kentucky　　　Barren County?
　　　Thornton, Presley,　　Male
The entry for land owned by Edmond Rogers was in his name.
Barren County Tax Book, 1800, part 1 - page: 13
FAMILY HISTORY LIBRARY film 7865
Tipton, Saml,　　Kentucky　　　Barren County?
　　　Tipton, Saml,　　Male
The entry for land owned by Henry Renick was in his name.
Barren County Tax Book, 1800, part 1 - page: 12
FAMILY HISTORY LIBRARY film 7865
Tony, John,　　Kentucky　　　Barren County?
　　　Tony, John,　　Male
The entry for land owned by Jacob Gipson was in his name.
Barren County Tax Book, 1800, part 1 - page: 6
FAMILY HISTORY LIBRARY film 7865
Trent, Brian,　　Kentucky　　　Barren County?
　　　Trent, Brian,　　Male
The entry for land owned by Jacob Clarke was in his name.
Barren County Tax Book, 1800, part 1 - page: 3
FAMILY HISTORY LIBRARY film 7865
Walker, Andrew,　　Kentucky　　　Barren County?
　　　Walker, Andrew,　　　Male

The entry for land owned by Jacob Clarke was in his name.
Barren County Tax Book, 1800, part 1 - page: 3
FAMILY HISTORY LIBRARY film 7865
Walker, Levi, Kentucky   Barren County?
        Walker, Levi,   Male
The entry for land owned by William Handy was in his name.
Barren County Tax Book, 1800, part 1 - page: 8
FAMILY HISTORY LIBRARY film 7865
Warren, D., Kentucky   Barren County?
        Warren, D.,   Male
The survey for land owned by William Feland was in the names of Wm Feland and D. Warren.
Barren County Tax Book, 1800, part 1 - page: 5
FAMILY HISTORY LIBRARY film 7865
Warren, David,   Kentucky   Barren County?
        Warren, David, Male
The entry for land owned by Samuel Renick senr was in his name.

Barren County Tax Book, 1800, part 1 - page: 13
FAMILY HISTORY LIBRARY film 7865
Wilson, Thos, Kentucky   Barren County?
        Wilson, Thos,   Male
The entry for land owned by Edmond Rogers was in his name.
Barren County Tax Book, 1800, part 1 - page: 13
FAMILY HISTORY LIBRARY film 7865
Wood, Absalom,.   Kentucky   Barren County?
        Wood, Absalom,   Male
The entry for land owned by David Hardin was in his name.
Barren County Tax Book, 1800, part 1 - page: 8
FAMILY HISTORY LIBRARY film 7865
Wood, Nathan,   Kentucky   Barren County?
        Wood, Nathan, Male
The entry for land owned by Moses Mitchel was in his name.
Barren County Tax Book, 1800, part 1 - page: 11
FAMILY HISTORY LIBRARY film 7865

STEMMONS PUBLISHING, 1078 Shields Lane, South Jordan, Utah 84095, 801-254-2152 (Call between 9:00 a.m. and 5:00 p.m. Monday through Friday. If no one answers, please leave a message.), stemmonspublishing@gmail.com

The importance of census records and other population lists cannot be overstated in terms of the help they are in locating people in a specific area. This allows one to examine other records in that area. This is one of our main goals and why we do business. What we are trying to accomplish is a work in progress. We hope to improve as we go along. Thank you for your patience.

Petitions are an important example of these population lists.

Thank you for the opportunity to serve you.

Sincerely,
John Stemmons

A COMPLETE LIST OF OUR GENEALOGY BOOKS

AL-01 **ALABAMA 1800 PETITIONERS [-1804]**© Compiled by John D Stemmons, 2021. This book compiled from *Territorial Papers of the United States* contains 253 entries for a very early period in Alabama's history. It may contain some biographical details and clues to prior residence. It can help substitute for the missing federal census. For information on how to obtain this book search by the title or "Books by John Stemmons" at Amazon.com. This comes automatically with a paperback binding. It includes but is not limited to petitions regarding:

- Seeking new territory due to the rapid migration from Georgia, etc.
- Petition seeking confirmation of land grants obtained from other governments.

36 Pages $7.20

AL-02 **ALABAMA 1810 PETITIONERS, ETC., [1805-1814]**© Compiled by John D Stemmons, 2021. This book compiled from *Territorial Papers of the United States* contains 1687 entries for a very early period in Alabama's history. It includes a census of

Madison County, taken Jan 1809. It may contain some biographical details and clues to prior residence. It can help substitute for the missing federal census. For information on how to obtain this book search by the title or "Books by John Stemmons" at Amazon.com. This comes automatically with a paperback binding. It includes but is not limited to petitions regarding:

- Issues relating to land.
- Petition of inhabitants east of Pearl River seeking to form a new territory.
- 1809 census of Madison County.
- Inhabitants of Tombigbee seeking for their purchases from the Spanish to be duty free at "Fort Stoddart".

176 Pages $35.20

AL-03 ALABAMA 1820 PETITIONERS, ETC., [1815-1824]©
Compiled by John D Stemmons, 2021. This book compiled from *Territorial Papers of the United States* contains 3913 entries for a fast-growing period in Alabama's history. It may contain some biographical details and clues to prior residence. It can help substitute for the missing federal census. For information on how to obtain this book search by the title or "Books by John Stemmons" at Amazon.com. This comes automatically with a paperback binding. It includes but is not limited to petitions regarding:

- Merchants and traders of St. Stephens seeking to establish that town as a port of delivery.
- Inhabitants of eastern part of MS territory, who lost much income/property in the wars with England & Indians.
- Inhabitants of Alabama Territory opposing the "settlements on the western side of the Mobile & Tombigby rivers" being made part of Mississippi.
- List of Letters, 9 Jan 1819, remaining in Huntsville Post Office.
- Issues about military and local officers.
- Memorial, ref. 20 Jan 1817, to Congress from inhabitants of Mobile complaining that Ft Charlotte is indefensible.

407 Pages $81.40

AR-01 ARKANSAS PETITIONERS, ETC. 1800, 1810 [1795-1814]© Compiled by John D Stemmons, 2021. This book compiled from *Territorial Papers of the United States* contains 261 entries and is a partial replacement for the missing federal censuses of 1800 and 1810. As a result, it is a very helpful resource in establishing residence of people in Arkansas during that early formative period in the state's history. These people include some of earliest you will find that established the foundation of what was to become the great state that Arkansas now is. This also makes it possible to determine what other records might be available for further research. Some additional biographical details may be included, and possible relationships with others may be revealed. For information on how to obtain this book search by the title or "Books by John Stemmons" at Amazon.com. This comes automatically with a paperback binding. It includes but is not limited to petitions regarding:

- Issues relating to land.
- Inhabitants of Arkansas District expressing concern about the hostile attitude of the Cherokees nearby.
- Issues about military and local officers.

43 Pages $8.60

AR-02 ARKANSAS PETITIONERS, ETC. 1820 [1815-1824]©
Compiled by John D Stemmons, 2021. This book compiled from *Territorial Papers of the United States* contains 1936 entries and is a partial replacement for the missing federal census of 1820. As a result, it is a very helpful resource in establishing residence of people in Arkansas during that fast-growing territorial period prior to becoming a state. Unfortunately, the 1820 census is not available to help track these people. That is why this new book can help. It is even better in some respects than the census because it helps us understand some of the challenges they faced. It also makes possible the determination of

other records that might be available for further research. Some additional biographical details may be included, and possible relationships with others may be revealed. Even the names of some Native Americans are included as well as a few potential residents of Oklahoma. For information on how to obtain this book search by the title or "Books by John Stemmons" at Amazon.com. This comes automatically with a paperback binding. It includes but is not limited to petitions regarding:

- Issues relating to land.
- Issues relating to Native Americans.
- Citizens of Arkansas County describing the good location of the Town of Arkansas.
- Appointments about military and local officers, etc.
- Inhabitants of Arkansas and Phillips Counties seeking a mail route from the Town of Arkansas to the "Post of Ouachita in Louisianna."
- Abstract of Grand and Petit Jurors, Oct term, 1824 listing compensation for their attendance at a Superior Court held at Little Rock.

216 Pages $43.20

1001-GEORGIA PETITIONS 1778-1784© Compiled by John D Stemmons, 2004. This book contains 256 entries for a very early period in Georgia's history. For information on how to obtain this book search by the title or "Books by John Stemmons" at Amazon.com. This comes automatically with a paperback binding. It includes but is not limited to petitions regarding:

- A desire for a new district.
- A request for local courts.
- Issues about military and local officers.
- Request for protection against enemies.
- A request for pardon, amnesty, etc.
- Description of hardship.

44 pages $8.80

1002-GEORGIA PETITIONS 1785-1794© Compiled by John D Stemmons, 2004. Contains 3720 entries which includes about 25% of the heads of household in Georgia at that time. As such this publication is an excellent substitute for the missing Georgia 1790 federal census. It even includes many names for Burke and Washington Counties which suffered severe record loss in the early years. For information on how to obtain this book search by the title or "Books by John Stemmons" at Amazon.com. This comes automatically with a paperback binding. It includes but is not limited to petitions regarding:

- Issues regarding local agencies, boundary changes, etc.
- Issues regarding religion and churches.
- Issues about military and local officers.
- Asking for measures to control slaves.
- Recommendation for a business opportunity.
- Seeking resolution of land problems, land fraud, etc.
- Asking for increased tobacco inspection fees.
- Request for protection against Indians.
- Issues about crimes, pardon, amnesty, etc.
- Description of hardship.

367 pages $73.40

IL-01 ILLINOIS PETITIONS, ETC., 1760-1810 [1755-1814]© Compiled by John D Stemmons, 2021, this book contains 3680 names from *The Territorial Papers of the U.S.* This covers a period of time even before the federal census of 1790. And while no federal censuses exists for Illinois from 1790-1810, these records nicely substitute for those missing documents. It should be noted that 1004-**A PARTIAL CENSUS FOR INDIANA TERRITORY 1810** includes most if not all the names for 1810. A study to determine that they were the same was inconclusive and so, just in the outside chance there might be some that were not the same, it was felt that they should be included. The convenience of having them together outweighs their exclusion.

These records include an incredible amount of information about these early people. One can see the change from a mostly French culture to that of English. The transition was not always peaceful. Included are census records, lists of inhabitants, and much more. While the federal censuses are missing that would help track these people, these records are even better in some respects than the census because it helps us understand some of the challenges they faced. That is why this new book can help. Some additional biographical details may be included, plus possible relationships with other family members. For information on how to obtain this book search by the title or "Books by John Stemmons" at Amazon.com. This comes automatically with a paperback binding. It includes but is not limited to petitions regarding:

- Issues relating to land.
- Issues relating to Native Americans.
- List of inhabitants at Kaskaskias before 1783.
- Appointments about military and local officers, etc.
- Lands claimed and possessed by inhabitants of the District of Cahokia on or before 1783 that still existed after 29 May 1790.
- Applications for lands in the District of Cahokia by persons claiming as settlers under the state of Virginia, if the settlements were made on or before 1783 that still existed after 29 May 1790.
- List of families at the Prairie du Pont, undated, but enclosed in St. Clair's report 10 Feb 1791.

349 Pages $69.80

IN-01 THE TERRITORY NORTHWEST OF THE RIVER OHIO, PETITIONERS, ETC., 1790-1800 [1785-1804] (Present day Indiana)© Compiled by John D Stemmons, 2021. This book was compiled from *Territorial Papers of the United States.* 1790 contains 242 names found on petitions, etc., including a census of heads of household for Vincennes. 1800 only includes 76 names and so is not as valuable as 1790. The population of Indiana would have increased significantly between 1790 and 1800. This is still a very early time prior to Indiana becoming a state. Unfortunately, there is no 1790 or 1800 census existing to help track these people. Therefore, we must do what we can with what is available. That is why this new book is so helpful. It is even better in some respects than the census because it helps us understand some of the challenges they faced. It also makes possible the determination of other records that might be available for further research such as land grants. Even the names of some Native Americans are listed. Some additional biographical details may be included, plus possible relationships with other family members. For information on how to obtain this book search by the title or "Books by John Stemmons" at Amazon.com. This comes automatically with a paperback binding. It includes but is not limited to petitions regarding:

- Issues relating to land.
- Heads of families settled at Post Vincennes on or before 1783 and residents at this time [13 Jul 1790] who are entitled to donation lands.
- Issues relating to Native Americans.
- Inhabitants of Vincennes who migrated to Vincennes around 1786 and received land, but never obtained a deed.
- Appointments about military and local officers, etc.

38 Pages $7.60

1003-INDIANA ELECTION RETURNS 1809, 1812© Compiled by John D and E. Diane Stemmons, 2004. This compilation of 3576 entries includes the names found in the territorial election returns which documents are in the Indiana Historical Society. Also included is a poll book of an election for Dearborn County in 1809 as found in *Territorial Papers of the United States.* All entries in this book are also found in *A Partial Census for Indiana Territory 1810.* The book *Indiana Election Returns, 1809, 1812* was compiled for just the election returns simply because they are one entire record source and may have some value in that. For information on how to obtain this

book search by the title or "Books by John Stemmons" at Amazon.com. This comes automatically with a paperback binding.
285 pages $57.00

1004-A PARTIAL CENSUS FOR INDIANA TERRITORY 1810© Compiled by John D and E. Diane Stemmons, 2021. With 8602 entries this book includes name lists found in *Territorial Papers of the United States* for Indiana Territory during the period 1805 through 1814. It also provides the names in *Indiana Election Returns 1809, 1812* listed above. Since there were approximately 4300 heads of households in the territory in 1810, *A Partial Census for Indiana Territory 1810* probably lists virtually every head of household in Indiana Territory for the time period. It makes an excellent substitute for the missing federal census for 1810. In addition, it includes names of people living in what is now Illinois, but which was part of Indiana Territory before 1809. Therefore, *A Partial Census for Indiana Territory 1810* is also a partial census of Illinois in the years between 1805 to 1809. For information on how to obtain this book search by the title or "Books by John Stemmons" at Amazon.com. This comes automatically with a paperback binding. It includes but is not limited to petitions regarding:

- Issues relating to land.
- Heads of families settled at Post Vincennes on or before 1783 and residents at this time [13 Jul 1790] who are entitled to donation lands.
- Issues relating to Native Americans.
- Inhabitants of Vincennes who migrated to Vincennes around 1786 and received land, but never obtained a deed.
- Appointments about military and local officers, etc.

574 pages $114.80

KY-01 KENTUCKY 1800, BARREN COUNTY TAX BOOK© Compiled by John D Stemmons, 2021. It contains 494 names from the Barren County tax list and 1 from *The Territorial Papers of the U.S.* Even though the 1800 census is missing this list it provides an amazing amount of information that substitutes nicely for that missing census, including white and black males aged 16-21 and those 21 and over. This is the kind of information one would expect to find on the census for that period. This list includes all taxable heads of household. Some additional biographical details may be included, plus possible relationships with other family members. The names of the blacks may be found in court, land, and probate records. For information on how to obtain this book search by the title or "Books by John Stemmons" at Amazon.com. This comes automatically with a paperback binding.
65 Pages $13.00

LA-01 ARKANSAS PETITIONS 1800 [1795-1804] and ORLEANS TERRITORY (NOW LOUISIANA) PETITIONS, ETC., 1800 [1795-1804]© Compiled by John D Stemmons, 2021. This book was compiled from *Territorial Papers of the United States* and contains 495 names for Louisiana and 3 from Arkansas. Since no federal census exists for Arkansas and Louisiana for 1800, these records nicely substitute for those missing documents. These records include an incredible amount of information about these early people. While the federal censuses are missing that would help track these people, these records are even better in some respects than the census because it helps us understand some of the challenges they faced. That is why this new book can help. Some additional biographical details may be included, plus possible relationships with other family members. For information on how to obtain this book search by the title or "Books by John Stemmons" at Amazon.com. This comes automatically with a paperback binding. It includes but is not limited to petitions regarding:

- Inhabitants of Pointe Coupee to Gov. Claiborne, requesting military aid because of fears of a slave revolt.
- Characterization of New Orleans residents, 1 July 1804.

- Address from the free people of color Jan. 1804, volunteering for military service.
- Memorial to Congress from merchants of New Orleans, 9 Jan 1804, offering allegiance to the US.
- Appointments about military and local officers, etc.

47 Pages $9.40

MO-01 MISSOURI PETITIONERS, ETC., 1780-1820 [1775-1824]© Compiled by John D Stemmons, 2021. This book was compiled from *Territorial Papers of the United States* and contains 1 name for 1780, 12 names for 1790, 19 names for 1800, 5057 names for 1810, and 1509 names for 1820. The later lists begin to approach the number needed to include most heads of household, and nicely substitute for missing or no censuses. These records include an incredible amount of information about these early people. While censuses help track people, the records this book includes are even better in some respects than the census because it helps us understand some of their personal feelings and challenges, they faced. Some additional biographical details may be included, plus possible relationships with other family members. For information on how to obtain this book search by the title or "Books by John Stemmons" at Amazon.com. This comes automatically with a paperback binding. It includes but is not limited to petitions, etc., regarding:

- Resolution recommending distinction between Americans and Frenchmen should be done away.
- Letter from U.S. President to Chief White Hairs and the warriors of the Osages, informing them of the Lewis and Clark expedition, and promising them a resident agent.
- Many petitions, etc., expressing their support and confidence in Governor Wilkinson. He was involved in scandals and controversies.
- Memorial recommending replacements for Governor Wilkinson.
- Petition expressing concern about changing the form of territorial government before they are adequately prepared.
- Memorial concerning the large number of their Spanish land claims that are being rejected.
- Lists of civil and military officers.
- Petition seeking a grant of a township of land for the support of the school as had been done in other areas.
- Petition seeking pre-emption rights for the services given in defending the frontier in Boon's Lick Settlement around 1815.
- Petitions relating to the New Madrid & Little Prairie earthquake.
- Petitions asking for new post offices and routes, etc.

552 pages $110.40

MI-01 MICHIGAN PETITIONS, ETC. 1790-1810 [1785-1814]© Compiled by John D Stemmons, 2021. This book was compiled from *Territorial Papers of the United States*. It contains 1 name for 1790, 794 names for 1800, and 1335 names for 1810. Clearly, that is not enough for 1790, but the others begin to approach the number needed. Especially is this so for 1810 because we are fortunate enough to have much of what appears to be the federal 1810 census. Since no federal census exists for 1800, these records nicely substitute for those missing documents. These records include an incredible amount of information about these early people. While censuses help track people, the records this book includes are even better in some respects than the census because it helps us understand some of their personal feelings and challenges, they faced. Some additional biographical details may be included, plus possible relationships with other family members. For information on how to obtain this book search by the title or "Books by John Stemmons" at Amazon.com. This comes automatically with a paperback binding. It includes but is not limited to petitions regarding:

- Inhabitants of Detroit seeking new territory because of distance to travel to the headquarters of Indiana Territory.

- Appointments about military and local officers, etc.
- Inhabitants of Wayne County seeking clarification of the status of their land.
- 1810 Census of the District of Detroit.
- Inhabitants of Michigan Ter. seeking time to file claims to their land.
- List, 23 Jul 1812, of patents received from the General Land Office for private claims in the District of Detroit.
- Petition from inhabitants of Michigan Territory asking that the new territorial code be printed also in French.
- Petition to Thomas Jefferson, from inhabitants of Michigan Territory complaining of Governor William Hull and Supreme Court Chief Justice Augustus B. Woodward.

222 Pages $44.40

MS-01 MISSISSIPPI TERRITORIAL PETITIONERS, ETC. 1800 [1795-1804]© Compiled by John D Stemmons, 2021. This book was compiled from *Territorial Papers of the United States and* contains 2566 names found on petitions, etc., from Mississippi Territory for this time period. This was during a fast-growing era prior to Mississippi becoming a state. Unfortunately, there is no 1800 census existing to help track these people. That is why this new book can help. It is even better in some respects than the census because it helps us understand some of the challenges they faced. It also makes possible the determination of other records that might be available for further research such as Spanish land grants. Some additional biographical details may be included, plus possible relationships with other family members. For information on how to obtain this book search by the title or "Books by John Stemmons" at Amazon.com. This comes automatically with a paperback binding. It includes but is not limited to petitions regarding:

- Citizens of territory asking land office to be in the area, settlers have pre-emption right, & suffrage be for males of age and US citizens & residents of territory for 6 months.
- Memorial by citizens of the territory, who obtained land before the area became part of the US.
- Testimonials, ca 1802, by individuals regarding the service of John Steele, secretary of the territory.
- Memorial by citizens of the territory seeking that "moderate grants [be] made to actual settlers on unappropriated lands,"
- Merchants of Natchez, complaining of the extra duties they must pay for merchandise shipped from the US.

209 Pages $41.80

MS-02 MISSISSIPPI TERRITORIAL PETITIONS, ETC. 1810 [1805-1814] and WEST FLORIDA 1820 PETITIONERS [1815-1824]© Compiled by John D Stemmons, 2021. This book was compiled from *Territorial Papers of the United States* and contains 1061 names found on petitions, etc., from Mississippi Territory for the period 1810 [1805-1814]. It also includes a list of 76 names on a petition to Congress, 11 Dec 1816, by inhabitants of Jackson County, Mississippi Territory, many of whom settled on land in West Florida while under Spanish control and now seek for their grant to be confirmed by the US. It is being included with Mississippi Territory because it is basically the same time period and place of residence. This was during a fast-growing time prior to Mississippi and Florida becoming states. Unfortunately, there is no 1810 or 1820 census existing to help track these people. That is why this new book can help. It is even better in some respects than the census because it helps us understand some of the challenges they faced. It also makes possible the determination of other records that might be available for further research. Some additional biographical details may be included, and possible relationships with others may be revealed. For information on how to obtain this book search by the title or "Books by John Stemmons" at Amazon.com. This comes automatically with a paperback binding. It includes but is not limited to petitions regarding:

- Inhabitants of the territory seeking adjustment of land claims obtained from the British Government.
- Inhabitants of the territory seek for a road to be built that follows the Pearl River which would shorten the route from Nashville to New Orleans.
- Inhabitants of Amite and Wilkinson Counties seek establishment of a post office.
- Memorial by citizens of the territory (Americans by birth?) seeking a postponement of statehood for the territory.
- Inhabitants of Jackson Co., Mississippi Territory, many of whom settled on land in West Florida while under Spanish control seek for their grant to be confirmed by the US.

108 Pages $21.60

NJ-01-NEW JERSEY PETITIONS 1740, 1745 THROUGH 1754©
Compiled by John D Stemmons, 2021. It contains 740 entries for a period of time in New Jersey when records are sparse. While that may not seem like very many names, it was during the time when the population was small, and the residence of people was sometimes hard to track. In looking through these petitions, it appears that the people of this era had basically the same concerns we have. One can see the forces of democracy beginning to stir that were to result in independence from Great Britain just a short three decades away. We can obtain a hint of the personal concerns of these people and what was important to them in this exciting historical time. Even at this time of great distress and hardship life had to go on. These petitions are almost like an open window into the lives of these people. For information on how to obtain this book search by the title or "Books by John Stemmons" at Amazon.com. This comes automatically with a paperback binding. It includes but is not limited to petitions regarding:
- Issues regarding exports and imports.
- Issues regarding devaluation of currency, money supply, etc.
- Issues regarding local agencies, boundary changes, etc.
- Seeking new legislation.
- Issues about military and government officers.
- Seeking resolution of land problems, etc.
- Protesting against the great number of taverns.
- Resolution of tax issues.
- Issues about crimes, pardon, amnesty, etc.

84 pages $16.80

NJ-02-NEW JERSEY PETITIONS 1755-1764© Compiled by John D Stemmons, 2004. Contains 2389 entries from many petitions submitted because of concerns about the French and Indian War. This book is an excellent census substitute. For information on how to obtain this book search by the title or "Books by John Stemmons" at Amazon.com. This comes automatically with a paperback binding. It includes petitions regarding:
- Issues regarding local agencies, boundary changes, etc.
- Issues about roads, bridges, etc.
- Opposition to importing slaves.
- Seeking naturalization.
- Seeking new legislation.
- Issues about military and government affairs.
- Request for reimbursement from the government.
- Request for protection against enemies.
- Seeking resolution of land problems, etc.
- Protesting against dispensing of "spirituous liquors"
- Issues about crimes, pardon, amnesty, etc.
- Description of hardship.

246 pages $49.20

NJ-03-NEW JERSEY PETITIONS 1765-1774© Compiled by John D Stemmons, 2004. This book contains 806 entries. While a small percent of the population, it represents the time leading up to the Revolution. For information on how to obtain this book search by the title or "Books by John Stemmons" at Amazon.com. This comes automatically with a paperback binding. It includes but is not limited to petitions regarding:
- Issues regarding agriculture, exports and imports.
- Request for permission to beg, financial support, etc.
- Issues about religion and churches.
- Request for medical standards.
- Issues regarding devaluation of currency, money supply, etc.
- Issues regarding local agencies, boundary changes, etc.
- Issues on hunting, fishing, etc.
- Issues about roads, bridges, etc.
- Issues relating to slavery.
- Issues about military and government affairs.
- Seeking resolution of land problems, etc.
- Issues about crimes, pardon, amnesty, etc.

99 pages $19.80

NJ-04-NEW JERSEY PETITIONS 1775-1784© Compiled by John D Stemmons, 2005. This book contains 6201 entries which is about 29% of the heads of household living in New Jersey at that time (not counting duplicate names.) It represents the historic period during the Revolution. For information on how to obtain this book search by the title or "Books by John Stemmons" at Amazon.com. This comes automatically with a paperback binding. It includes but is not limited to petitions regarding:
- Issues regarding trade, exports, and imports.
- Issues regarding devaluation of currency, money supply, price controls, etc.
- Issues on religion and churches.
- Issues regarding local agencies, boundary changes or disputes, etc.
- Issues on court cases.
- Request for guardianship of children.
- Issues about roads, bridges, canals, etc.
- Issues on slavery.
- Seeking new legislation or repealing old laws.
- Issues about military and government affairs and officers.
- Issues about payment from the government.
- Issues on independence and the Revolutionary War.
- Request for protection against enemies.
- Seeking resolution of property and land problems, etc.
- Issues about crimes, pardon, amnesty, etc.
- Resolution of tax issues.

559 pages $111.80

NJ-05-NEW JERSEY PETITIONS 1785-1794 Volumes 1-2©
Compiled by John D Stemmons, 2005. This book contains 10,353 entries which covers about 35% of the heads of household for that time, not counting duplicate names. For information on how to obtain this book search by the title or "Books by John Stemmons" at Amazon.com. This comes automatically with a paperback binding. It includes but is not limited to petitions regarding:
- Economic issues regarding the devaluation of currency, public debt, etc.
- Issues on religion and churches.
- Issues regarding counties and towns, etc.
- Issues on court cases.
- Issues regarding hunting on private property, fishing, etc.
- Issues about roads, bridges, canals, ferries, etc.
- Issues relating to schools.
- Issues on slavery.
- Seeking new legislation or repealing existing laws.
- Issues about military and government affairs and officers.
- Seeking payment from the government.

- Expressing approval of the U.S. Constitution.
- Seeking resolution of property and land problems, etc.
- Issues about crimes, pardon, amnesty, etc.
- Resolution of tax issues.

Volume 1, A Through K, pages 462	$92.40
Volume 2, L Through Z, pages 470	$94.00

NJ-06 NEW JERSEY PETITIONERS, ETC., 1800 [1795-1804] Volumes 1-3© Compiled by John Stemmons, 2021. All volumes of this book contain 13,144 names. Unlike the tax ratables, these records cover the entire state for the period just after the Revolutionary War These records provide a place of residence which can lead to other records to search. For information on how to obtain this book search by the title or "Books by John Stemmons" at Amazon.com. This comes automatically with a paperback binding. It includes but is not limited to petitions regarding:

- Public buildings including poor house, taverns, banks, etc.
- Issues on religion and churches.
- Issues regarding counties and towns, etc.
- Issues on court cases.
- Concerning voting opportunities
- Issues about roads, bridges, canals, ferries, water rights, storage of gunpowder, etc.
- Issues relating to schools.
- Issues on slavery.
- Seeking new legislation or repealing existing laws.
- Issues about military and government affairs and officers.
- Seeking payment from the government.
- Seeking resolution of property and land problems, etc.
- Issues about crimes, pardon, amnesty, etc.
- Resolution of tax issues.

Volume 1, A Through E, pages 423	$84.60
Volume 2, F Through R, pages 529	$105.80
Volume 3, S Through Z, pages 358	$71.60

NJ-07 NEW JERSEY TAX RATABLES, 1770 [1765-1774] This book contains 2373 names of those who are taxable. They do include important details about the property they held and may provide clues regarding relationship, etc. For information on how to obtain this book search by the title or "Books by John Stemmons" at Amazon.com. This comes automatically with a paperback binding.

250 pages	$50.00

NJ-08 NEW JERSEY TAX RATABLES, 1780 [1775-1784] This book contains 4358 names of those who are taxable. It includes important details about the property they held and may provide clues regarding relationship, etc. For information on how to obtain this book search by the title or "Books by John Stemmons" at Amazon.com. This comes automatically with a paperback binding.

440 pages	$88.00

NJ-09 NEW JERSEY TAX RATABLES, 1790 [1785-1794] This book contains 2307 names of those who are taxable. Unfortunately, Burlington and Cape May counties are not covered by this period. We are fortunate though in have the petitions that cover the same time. It is interesting to compare the two sets of records. They were not combined because that would make the books too large. The tax ratables do include important details about the property they held and may provide clues regarding relationship, etc. For information on how to obtain this book search by the title or "Books by John Stemmons" at Amazon.com. This comes automatically with a paperback binding.

268 pages	$53.60

NJ-10 NEW JERSEY TAX RATABLES, 1800 [1795-1804] , Volumes 1-2 This book contains 8396 names of those who are taxable. It includes important details about the property they held and may provide clues regarding relationship, etc. For information on how

to obtain this book search by the title or "Books by John Stemmons" at Amazon.com. This comes automatically with a paperback binding.

Volume 1, A Through K, pages 456	$91.20
Volume 2, L Through Z, pages 449	$89.80

NC-01 NORTH CAROLINA PETITIONERS, ETC. 1780 [1775-1784]© Compiled by John Stemmons, 2021. This book contains 4866 names and was assembled from records located at the North Carolina State Archives. This was before the federal census was taken and is a valuable resource for locating people in this early time. Included are some names from what is now, Tennessee. For information on how to obtain this book search by the title or "Books by John Stemmons" at Amazon.com. This comes automatically with a paperback binding.

- Economic issues regarding the devaluation of currency, public debt, etc.
- Issues on religion and churches.
- Issues regarding counties and towns, etc.
- Issues regarding hunting on private property, fishing, etc.
- Issues about roads, bridges, canals, ferries, etc.
- Seeking new legislation or repealing existing laws.
- Issues about military and government affairs and officers.
- Seeking resolution of property and land problems, etc.
- Issues about crimes, pardon, amnesty, etc.

568 pages	$113.60

1009-ROWAN COUNTY, NORTH CAROLINA TAX LISTS 1758/1759, 1761, 1768, 1778, 1779© Compiled by John D and E. Diane Stemmons, 2004. This publication serves as a census for Rowan County for about three decades which includes two major conflicts, the French and Indian and Revolutionary wars. Thus, one may be able to track individuals that stayed in the county over a significant period of time. Sometimes sons and slaves are given plus other important information. These tax lists are listed alphabetically in three separate sections.

218 pages	$43.60

OH-01 TERRITORY NW OF OHIO RIVER, PETITIONERS, ETC. 1790-1800 [1785-1804] (Now Ohio)© Compiled by John D Stemmons, 2021. It contains 217 names for 1790 and 3047 names for 1800. This book may include many heads of household at that time and serves as a substitute for missing or no censuses. It even incorporates the names of many native Americans. These records provide an incredible amount of information about these early people. While censuses help track people, the records this book contains are even better in some respects than the census because it helps us understand some of their personal information not recorded by a census. Some additional biographical details may be included, plus possible relationships with other family members. For information on how to obtain this book search by the title or "Books by John Stemmons" at Amazon.com. This comes automatically with a paperback binding. It includes but is not limited to petitions regarding:

- Petition of the French inhabitants of Gallipolis regarding their purchase of lands from the Scioto Company.
- Inhabitants on the Muskingum to Governor St. Clair.
- Petitions about land and issues with John Cleves Symmes.
- 1800, Population Schedules, Washington County. Territory Northwest of the River Ohio.
- Petition by inhabitants telling of losses in the "Late Indian war" and their inability to obtain land in Kentucky.
- Petition by inhabitants of Hamilton County seeking approval to purchase reserved land in order to build a grist mill because it has a sufficient stream of water.
- List of Gallipolis proprietors and the amount of their land purchases.

285 pages	$57.00

PA-01 PENNSYLVANIA CHESTER COUNTY TAX LIST 1771© Compiled by John D Stemmons, 2021. It contains 5621 names. This

record lists all taxable people in the county, and as such, is a good census substitute. It is not known what is meant by the abbreviations or "inmate". Perhaps they were incarcerated in jail or were indentured in some way. Often an occupation is listed. Occasionally there will be information about family relationships. It is helpful that this book includes the information about the taxable property. For information on how to obtain this book search by the title or "Books by John Stemmons" at Amazon.com. This comes automatically with a paperback binding.
399 pages $79.80

South Carolina

South Carolina has a remarkable series of records that makes it unique for the Colonial period. These are the "Jury Lists" compiled by the government to function as a list of names from which members of a jury could be assigned. They cover the period 1720-1783 and, according to the act in 1731, were compiled from tax lists of the preceding year [which no longer exist], listing every person who paid a tax of twenty shillings or more. Those who paid five pounds or more were listed as grand jurors. The poorer class of people would not be listed. While not a complete list of the heads of household, they represent a sizeable proportion. They serve as a census during a period of growth, migration, and war. Usually only the name is given, but sometimes an occupation or name of the father is listed, etc. Many names are on more than one list for a particular year.

1010-**SOUTH CAROLINA 1720 JURY LIST**© Compiled by John D and E. Diane Stemmons, 2004. This publication has 840 entries covering a time when South Carolina was only 50 years old and the population was very small with only an estimated 885 heads of household. Unfortunately, it does not list a residence other than South Carolina. For information on how to obtain this book search by the title or "Books by John Stemmons" at Amazon.com. This comes automatically with a paperback binding.
48 pages $9.60

1017-**SOUTH CAROLINA 1731 JURY LIST**© Compiled by John D and E. Diane Stemmons, 2005. This book contains 2160 entries. It lists the locality of every person. For information on how to obtain this book search by the title or "Books by John Stemmons" at Amazon.com. This comes automatically with a paperback binding.
110 pages $22.00

1011-**SOUTH CAROLINA 1740 JURY LIST**© Compiled by John D and E. Diane Stemmons, 2004. This book contains 2160 entries. It lists the locality of every person. For information on how to obtain this book search by the title or "Books by John Stemmons" at Amazon.com. This comes automatically with a paperback binding.
111 pages $22.20

1012-**SOUTH CAROLINA 1751 JURY LIST**© Compiled by John D and E. Diane Stemmons, 2004. This book contains 2170 entries. It lists the locality of every person. For information on how to obtain this book search by the title or "Books by John Stemmons" at Amazon.com. This comes automatically with a paperback binding.
109 pages $21.80

1013-**SOUTH CAROLINA 1757 JURY LIST**© Compiled by John D and E. Diane Stemmons, 2004. This book contains 2624 entries. It lists the locality of every person. For information on how to obtain this book search by the title or "Books by John Stemmons" at Amazon.com. This comes automatically with a paperback binding.
135 pages $27.00

1014-**SOUTH CAROLINA 1767 JURY LIST**© Compiled by John D and E. Diane Stemmons, 2004. This book contains 2385 entries. It lists the locality of every person. For information on how to obtain this book search by the title or "Books by John Stemmons" at Amazon.com. This comes automatically with a paperback binding.

127 pages $25.40

SC-07 SOUTH CAROLINA 1780 [1775-1784], VOLUMES 1-2© Compiled by John D Stemmons, 2021. It contains 13,444 names. This record of jury lists consist of many people during the Colonial/Revolutionary War period and as such, is a good census substitute. Since Loyalists owned property that they paid taxes on, they may be included as well. These records provide a place of residence which can lead to other records to search. For information on how to obtain this book search by the title or "Books by John Stemmons" at Amazon.com. This comes automatically with a paperback binding.
Volume 1, 502 pages $100.40
Volume 2, 575 pages $115.00

TN-01 TENNESSEE PETITIONS, ETC., 1770-1790 [1765-1794]© Also known as Territory South of Ohio River. Compiled by John Stemmons, 2021. This book was assembled from *Territorial Papers of the United States* and contains 1 name for 1770, 12 names for 1780, and 1161 names for 1790 These people listed seem to be the more prominent persons, so, most of the less noteworthy individuals would not be listed. Still, the people listed clarify this early time before Tennessee became a state. The amount of biographical information is significant compared to the other books we have compiled from *Territorial Papers of the United States*. Many Native American names are included. For information on how to obtain this book search by the title or "Books by John Stemmons" at Amazon.com. This comes automatically with a paperback binding. It includes but is not limited to petitions regarding:

- "One of twelve men selected by the Cumberland people to govern the settlement, 1783; appointed by the Governor of North Carolina judge of the courts, Davidson County, 1783.
- Appointments about military and local officers, etc.
- Name on the "Treaty of Holston", 2 Jul 1791 between the President of the US and "Chiefs and Warriors of the Cherokee Nation of Indians."
- Memorial, 1 Aug 1791, to the President from the civil and military officers of Mero District explaining recent depredations of the Indians and seeking an "Act of Cession" from North Carolina.

95 pages $19.00

TN-02 TENNESSEE PETITIONERS, ETC. AND GRAINGER COUNTY TAX LISTS 1800 [1795-1804]© Compiled by John Stemmons, 2021. Also known as Territory South of Ohio River. This book was assembled from Grainger County Tax Lists 1800 and *Territorial Papers of the United States* and contains 182 names for the *Papers* and 247 names for the tax lists. From *Territorial Papers of the United States* the names mostly seem to be persons appointed to official or military positions or are members of the Knoxville Convention. Thus, they seem to be the more prominent persons, so, most of the less noteworthy individuals would not be listed. Still, the people listed clarify this early time before Tennessee became a state. The tax lists record the names of those who are taxable and are much more inclusive. They do include important details about the property they held. For information on how to obtain this book search by the title or "Books by John Stemmons" at Amazon.com. This comes automatically with a paperback binding. It includes but is not limited to petitions regarding:

- List, 21 Dec 1795, of members of Knoxville Convention.
- Appointments of military and local officers, etc.

49 pages $9.80

TN-03 TENNESSEE GRAINGER COUNTY TAX LISTS 1810 [1805-1814]© Compiled by John Stemmons, 2021. This book was assembled from Grainger County Tax Lists 1810 and contains 1242 names of those who are taxable. They do include important details about the property they held and may provide clues regarding

relationship, etc. For information on how to obtain this book search by the title or "Books by John Stemmons" at Amazon.com. This comes automatically with a paperback binding.
146 pages $29.20

TN-04 TENNESSEE GRAINGER COUNTY TAX LISTS 1820 [1815-1824]© Compiled by John Stemmons, 2021. This book was assembled from Grainger County Tax Lists 1820 and contains 1161 names of those who are taxable. They do include important details about the property they held and may provide clues regarding relationship, etc. The lists for 1800-1820 furnish an excellent opportunity to track the population growth of the county. For information on how to obtain this book search by the title or "Books by John Stemmons" at Amazon.com. This comes automatically with a paperback binding.
131 pages $26.20

VA-01 VIRGINIA PERSONAL PROPERTY TAX LISTS, 1780 [1775-1784] (Accomack and Albemarle Counties)© Compiled by John Stemmons, 2021. This book was assembled from Accomack and Albemarle Counties Personal Property Tax Lists ca 1780 and contains 2553 names of those who are taxable. They do include important details about the property they held and may provide clues regarding relationship, etc. They even furnish the entry for, it is assumed, future president Thomas Jefferson! For information on how to obtain this book search by the title or "Books by John Stemmons" at Amazon.com. This comes automatically with a paperback binding.
252 pages $50.40

VA-02 VIRGINIA PERSONAL PROPERTY TAX LISTS, 1790 [1785-1794] (Accomack and Albemarle Counties)© Compiled by John Stemmons, 2021. This book was assembled from Accomack and Albemarle Counties Personal Property Tax Lists ca 1790 and contains

2679 names of those who are taxable, plus 3 from *Territorial Papers of the U.S.* They do include important details about the property they held and may provide clues regarding relationship, etc. They even furnish the entry for, it is assumed, future president Thomas Jefferson! Data on the age range of males is also included. For information on how to obtain this book search by the title or "Books by John Stemmons" at Amazon.com. This comes automatically with a paperback binding.
333 pages $66.60

VA-03 VIRGINIA PERSONAL PROPERTY TAX LISTS, ca 1800 [1795-1804] (Accomack and Albemarle Counties)© Compiled by John Stemmons, 2021. This book was assembled from Accomack and Albemarle Counties Personal Property Tax Lists ca 1800 and contains 3788 names of those who are taxable. They do include important details about the property they held and may provide clues regarding relationship, etc. They even furnish the entry for, it is assumed, future president Thomas Jefferson! Data on the age range of males is also included. With the lists for 1780-1800 one can track population growth in these countries. An individual showing up for the first time may indicate potential age. For information on how to obtain this book search by the title or "Books by John Stemmons" at Amazon.com. This comes automatically with a paperback binding.
436 pages $87.20

Population estimates were obtained from U.S. Bureau of the Census, *Historical Statistics of the United States, Colonial Times to 1957,* Washington, D.C., 1960, Library of Congress Card No. A 60-9150; and United States. Bureau of the Census, *A Century of Population Growth From the First Census of the United States to the Twelfth, 1790-1900* Washington: Government Printing Office, 1909. A household size of 5.7 persons was assumed.

Good morning.
We received the gift book of "Georgia Petitions 1785-1794". Fantastic book and a great tool in researching that time period. I like the format which is easy to read and puts in one place the petitions for research. I personally have searched many of the petitions and love this new tool. The introduction and the list of petitions gives much added information to understanding the petitions for the various individuals.
I look forward to ordering more books in July after our budget is in place. Thank you for contacting our library and making us aware of your fine publications. Have a great day.
Thanks,
Irene Godwin
Ellen Payne Odom Genealogy Library
204 5th St. S.E.
P.O. Box 2828
Moultrie, GA 31768

EXAMPLES OF THE KIND OF INFORMATION CONTAINED IN OUR BOOKS

Cicotte, J. Bte.,   Michigan Territory, District of Detroit, "Cote des Poux"

Cicotte, J. Bte.,	45-Over?	Male	**Color:**	White
10-16	Male	**Color:**	White
10-16	Male	**Color:**	White
16-26	Male	**Color:**	White
45-Over	Female	**Color:**	White

1810 Census of the District of Detroit
MS/Witherell (B. F. H.) Collection, LMS, Burton Historical Collection, Detroit Public Library, Folder 2
Cicotte, Jacques,   Michigan Territory
     Cicotte, Jacques,   Male
Petition, 26 Oct 1807, to Congress from inhabitants of Michigan Ter. seeking time to file claims to their land, claims on 1+ parcels be confirmed, farms on Detroit River be extended to 80 arpents, & occupancy later than 1 Jul 1796 be allowed [pp. 138-49].
Territorial Papers of the US - volume: 10 page: 146
Holeday, Jas,   Territory NW of Ohio River   Knox County, Vincennes
     Holeday, Jas,   Male
Address to Colonel Josiah Harmar by American inhabitants of Post Vincennes dated 4 Aug 1787
Territorial Papers of US - volume: 2 page: 65
Holliday, Heirs of James,   Territory NW of Ohio River   Knox County, Vincennes
     Holliday, Heirs of James,   Male

Petition, 7 Aug 1797, to Congress by inhabitants of Knox County, who migrated to Vincennes around 1786 and received land, but never obtained a deed.
Territorial Papers of US - volume: 2 page: 621
Lajoye, Pierre ,   Spanish North America, St. Louis
        Lajoye, Pierre,   Male
        "Pierre Lajoye, formerly of Prairie du Rocher on the American side of the Mississippi".
Letter, 1790, by Governor St. Clair to Manuel Perez concerning an American boy in the possession of Pierre Lajoye [pages 237-238].
"Mr. Mayet has just complained to me that a Mr. La Joye, to whom he has entrusted an American boy, whom he took from the savages, to be returned to the parents of the latter, has not returned him, but is holding the boy as a slave and refuses to return the boy to them on the pretext of some debt. I am convinced that you will not find it proper that a free child should be held as a slave for the debts of another--and will order Mr. La Joye to return him to Mayet."
Letter, 26 May 1790, from St. Louis by Manuel Perez to Governor St. Clair concerning an American boy in the possession of Pierre Lajoye [pages 237-240]:
"MY DEAR SIR: In order to take cognizance of the subject of the claim in your favor of the 20th instant concerning the child who is today in the possession of Mr. Lajoye, I had the latter appear before me and from the questions which I put to him and the reasons which he advanced to me on this subject I have found in him only a disposition to render service to the Unhappy Father who lost him and who asks for him in a letter of which the said Mr. Lajoye is the bearer.

After studying this matter carefully, I find that the above-mentioned child claimed by Mr. Mayet can leave the possession of Mr. Lajoye only to go to that of the Father now living at Natches. I think also that it is just for the said Mr. Mayet to be reimbursed for what he actually gave the savages in order to get him out of their barbarous hands; . . .

When the young man arrived at Mr. Lajoye's house, he came and notified me of it at once and that he would write to the lower part of the Colony to learn in what district the Father of the said child lived. He learned later from the letter of which he is the bearer, that he resides at Natchez; accordingly he will send him down on the first opportunity."
Territorial Papers of the US - volume: 2 page: 237
Mayfield, Geddeon, Kentucky Barren County
        Mayfield, Geddeon,   Male
Acres of land: 200; Barren Co.; watercourse: Mill Creek; Entry: Geddeon Mayfield; Survey: same; Patent: 0; white males over 21: 0; white males 16-21: 0; blacks over 16: 0; total blacks: 0; horses: 0; stud horses: 0; retail stores: 0; tavern license: 0.
Barren County Tax Book, 1800, part 1 - page: 10 FAMILY HISTORY LIBRARY film 7865

LEGISLATIVE PETITIONS

Petitions to the governor, legislature, etc., were a particularly important way for individuals to communicate with their government regarding issues that were very essential to them. Their influence in making changes throughout our history has contributed to making our society what it is today. They are an important link in our legislative and judicial history. In these early petitions one can trace the growing desire for democracy. In fact, they are one of the most visible manifestations of democracy in practice. It is fascinating to view the changes in the reasons for submitting petitions over time (see the lists below.)

Because petitions represent the feelings of one or more individuals, they provide a window into the soul of the petitioners that illuminates the historical landscape. Most aspects of the human condition are addressed in some form by these important documents. The names listed with the petition can be used as a census of inhabitants for a particular locality. Often it is possible to determine useful information about individual persons from these records. They can help compensate for lost or destroyed county records. Petitions are original records that contain historical background about our culture and society.

Unfortunately, petitions are among the most inaccessible and underused records because there are so many, they are often difficult and time-consuming to read, and are usually housed only in the state archives or other repository in their un-microfilmed condition.

To help resolve this problem, we have abstracted the content of many petitions and indexed the names of the petitioners. A brief context of the petition is provided with each name. Generally, we have not included those petitions with fewer than 10-12 names.

GENEALOGY AND LOCAL HISTORY BOOKS IN PDF FORMAT ON A FLASH DRIVE

705 Local and Family History books for $75-or 11 cents a book!!! All 4 volumes of Savage's Genealogical Dictionary of New England would cost you about $0.44!*
You can have in your library/home more books of this type than most libraries have. They cover nearly all aspects of human experience including law, medicine, biography, history, etc., etc.

Concerns?
1. **Question:** I am uncomfortable in letting patrons use this small drive as it may become lost.

Answer: Simply download the contents of the drive onto your computer(s) and keep the drive in a safe place. We will replace it at no charge if it becomes lost.

2. **Question:** Some of our books, including those on microfilm, that are also on your flash drive are in poor condition because of patron use through the years, especially when copies are made. Copies made from microfilm are not always the best quality. How can you help us with these problems?

Answer: Once our books are on your computers, your originals can be kept in a secured area so that no more damage will occur because of hands-on use. The images on the computer can be easily printed, usually with better quality.

3. **Question:** We are only interested in items covering the locality our patrons live in.

Answer: Many of your patrons were born outside of your area and/or have ancestry from all over the United States, etc.

4. **Question:** Are these books under copyright restrictions?

Answer: They are in the public domain and so are not copyrightable.

Approximately how many pages do the 705 books add up to?

Total cost (from Stemmons Publishing) for hard copies: $7044 (not available now)

Approximated total pages of text on the flash drive: 221,307

Approximated total images on the flash drive: 58,272

A huge genealogical library of 705 books on your computer for only $75

A dealer's discount is available of $45 for 5 or more flash drives.

Imagine 705 books… 60,417 images… 230,642 pages on a small flash drive.

You may be able to find these books on Google, Ancestry, or FamilySearch. To make a hard copy from these sources may be expensive, especially if you were to copy all 705! I may be mistaken, but I'm not sure you can print just a single page from those services. You can with my books. You also have them immediately at your fingertips without needing to go to the effort to search these other services.

The downside to these books is that many are not indexed.

No problem: just check the index provided by these other sources before using our books.

"In 2016, popular genealogy blogger Dick Eastman surmised that perhaps ninety percent of the resources you may need to fill out your family tree are not yet available on the Internet." This statement was found on the Boston Public Library website. If that is true, some of the books on our flash drive may not be found on the Internet.

You may obtain a copy of the drive by sending check, money order, or cash to John Stemmons at 1078 Shields Lane, South Jordan, Utah, 801-254-2152 (Call between 9:00 a.m. and 5:00 p.m. Monday through Friday. If no one answers, please leave a message.), stemmonspublishing@gmail.com. We have been in this business since 1975! Check BBB if you need to.

The fee for shipping and handling is $10.00 unless you send a shipping container, deliverable to you, with sufficient postage to mail to you. Please allow 4-6 weeks for delivery.

The books on the drive are in the public domain and are not copyrighted. You may make as many copies of them as you would like. Please do not place the contents of the drive, in part or in full, on the Internet except for individual pages.

We do not do credit cards and PayPal. If you are unhappy with the drive, please return it for a refund of your money.

If you would like a list of questions and answers or a list of the books, please let us know.

*How are we able to do this? Simply by reducing each page so that 2-6 pages can be placed on a single 8½ by 11 sheet of paper and still be readable. With the computer, you can enlarge it as many times as needed.

Number of books by locality:

US-99, Regional-32, AL-1, CT-31, DE-1, GA-2, IL-1, IN-1, KY-1, ME-23, MD-15, MA-91, MI-1, MN-1, MO-2, NH-20, NJ-28, NY-81, NC-9, OH-9, PA-51, RI-6, SC-26, VT-2, VA-47, WV-1; Family History-62; CN-5; EN-39; IR-10; SCOT-7=705 books!